YOU SAY
to·ma·to

ALSO BY R. W. JACKSON

The Diabolical Dictionary of Modern English

YOU SAY
to · ma · to

An Amusing and Irreverent Guide
to the Most Often Mispronounced Words
in the English Language

R. W. JACKSON

THUNDER'S MOUTH PRESS

NEW YORK

YOU SAY TOMATO
An Amusing and Irreverent Guide to the Most Often
Mispronounced Words in the English Language

Published by
Thunder's Mouth Press
An Imprint of Avalon Publishing Group
245 West 17th Street, 11th Floor
New York, NY 10011

AVALON
publishing group incorporated

Copyright © 2005 by R. W. Jackson

First printing September 2005

Library of Congress Cataloging-in-Publication Data is available.

ISBN: 1-56025-762-8

9 8 7 6 5 4 3 2 1

Book design by Jamie McNeely

Printed in the United States
Distributed by Publishers Group West

For my wife and the Colonel

For my family, living and not so living

To the memory of the Giants:
Samuel Johnson and A. G. Bierce,
the latter whose masterwork's centennial
is observed in 2006

fore·word

So you thought "victual" was pronounced as *VIK-chew-ul*, did you? And "forte" is pronounced as *for-TAY*, right? Well, for "bettor" (*BET-ur*) or for "worsted" (*WOOS-tid*), R. W. Jackson will guide you, amusingly (that is the intention), through the murky phonological corridors where words such as "Aesop" and "anchovy," "gyro" and "synecdoche" lie in wait to trip the tongue fantastic.

Fresh from his post as activities director for the Cryonics Institute, Jackson will hold you spellbound and incredulous as his lambastinous lexicon looks at the many twists and turns language and pronunciation have taken in the last few generations.

Of the more than five hundred thousand words in the English language, here are seven hundred or so (count 'em yourself—I didn't have time to) of the most frequently mispronounced, complete with their somewhat uninhibited, though attractively styled, definitions.

The need for such a work is obvious. Even now, our president's emphasis is on education. And, as we all know, he could use a little. The man is not above slurring his words and unintentionally malaproping his way through press conferences to the chuckles of thousands, à la Dan Quayle. But the president knows that education is of prime importance in a civilized society: bringing college entrants up to at least an eighth-grade reading level; teaching engineering students fractions; getting our social studies teachers off the streets, etc. All the while, our great nation reels from war, economic uncertainty, lack of leadership, fiscal irresponsibility, and the threat of another Rolling Stones tour. What a guy!

So as the ugly wheels of time turn, let us retreat to the propriety and decorum that distinguished those great pronunciators of yore: William Jennings Bryan, Franklin Delano Roosevelt, Mel Tillis. Armed with the peculiar knowledge and exact information contained in this rousing little volume, you are sure to become a repository of the ultimate utterance, not to mention an indefatigable source of conversational interruptions wherever you go.

Placed strategically near other indispensable tomes such as *Roget's Thesaurus*, *Webster's 3rd Unabridged*, and the *Playboy Bartender's Guide*, this invaluable work will round out anyone's library of required references.

C. Lector Prndl, M.A., D.Litt.
Ann Arbor, Michigan

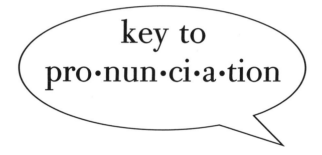

key to pro·nun·ci·a·tion

See exhibits A through Z.

au·thor's war·ning

Warning! Everyday use of the correct pronunciations contained in this dictionary may cause you to be accused of, among other things, "speaking in tongues," cipher networking, or otherwise being connected with the vanguard of an extraterrestrial force, by such people as roofers, cotillion planners, personal trainers, quail hunters, bodybuilders, motor pool sergeants, skinheads, focus groupies, 4-wheelers, toenail readers, or past, present, or future audience members of any TV talk show requiring them to wear bibs, body armor, and crash helmets. It would be wise of you to let slip an occasional *"WURST-uh-shi-er,"* *"EL-mund,"* or (God help us!) *"ASH-fawlt"* . . . lest you attract the felonious wrath of the clinically suspicious.

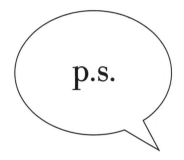

For TV and/or film rights to this work, please contact the author through the address of the publisher.

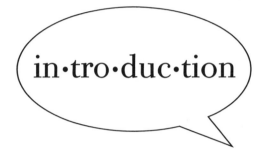

in·tro·duc·tion

The public outcry demanding a new dictionary of
English pronunciation, which began in the streets of
New Haven, Cambridge, Berkeley, and Tuba City in
mid-2003 and has since caused a general tumult
throughout what's left of the civilized world, resulting
in the terrible rioting by assistant librarians, head-
waiters of internet cafes, and resident onomasticians
of "American Universities" from Bhutan to Beirut, as
well as the equally ugly demonstrations staged by

sympathetic nonfiction typesetters in Visby and ranking ex-Party proofreaders of the Soviet Republic of Georgia (now called "Highland Park"), will hopefully (in the best sense of disjunction) be appeased by this grand work.

Following the lead of the usual indicators suggesting linguistic and/or pronunciatic decline, such as the promiscuous use of exclamation points, ellipses, and semicolons below the twenty-eighth parallel; the curious absence of the subjunctive in women's kickboxing commentary; the Supreme Court's ruling that free speech will cost $1.99 beginning with fiscal year 2014; the reported increase in intentional belching at Swarthmore alumni reunions; the appearance of English subtitles on MTV Awards Night telecasts beamed to the UK and Vermont; the ascendancy of chin stubble, especially in males; the epidemic of ADD (Adverb Deficit Disorder); the introduction of a hiphop version of the *Unabridged Oxford English Dictionary*, on two CDs; the thong-underwear scandal involving Visiting Lecturer Sir Malcolm Bestbuoy at the Passaic chapter of the Queen's English Society; the alarming dip in tuxedo sales worldwide; the clandestine purchase of automobile sub-woofers by freshmen congressmen;

and the spike in tattoo parlor openings nationally, to name a few, I determined that the time was right to put forth *You Say Tomato*.

Lest I be remiss in citations, the *positive* occurrences in recent language and usage are: a) the appearance, in 2004, of a *multisyllabic* R-rated Hollywood screenplay; b) the delivery of an emergency ration of twelve copies of *The Elements of Style* to the U.N. Security Council; and c) the change in spelling of the word "nuclear," to "nookyuhlur" by executive order, nay, presidential mandate, in 2001.

While it is always gratifying for a writer to be able to offer a fresh reference book, it is even more satisfying to present one totally up-to-date and devoted to the wealth of exquisite and unusual words and expressions with which the corpus of English speech, as well as writing, has been endowed over the centuries, by current has-beens as well as past.

A smattering of worthy non-English entries is also included here, either because such words are of particular interest in a derivative sense or they were needed to expand the volume to the minimum 1½" thickness expected of the better class of semi-scholarly publications. The dead languages—

Latin, Aramaic, Beatnikic, etc.—alas, shall not be represented, unless authorized by Mel Gibson.

In all instances, terseness of entry was given prime consideration by the author (or somewhat vitriolically "suggested" by his editors), in order to allow easy assimilation by the modern reader, whose receptors, it is commonly acknowledged, have been honed to an exceedingly fine edge by traffickers in soundbite TV, the Regents of the Cliffs Notes Society, the commandants of subdivisional latchkey orphanages, the interdictors of preschool grammar primers, and the agents of instant *Glace de Viande* and potato pancakes in a box, but was ultimately rejected.

With regard to the content and structure of the book, the author received no assistance, contributions, entries, or suggestions whatsoever from several sources: 1. Internationally recognized wordplay gurus; 2. Internet grammar aficionados; 3. Several incarcerated assistant professors of English convicted of wire fraud; 4. Literary agents; 4.5. Selected fellows of the Oakbrook, IL, Society of Nude Polka Dancers; 4.75. The League of Logomachians; and 5. Inadequately entreated chieftains of language whose own edgeless literary strivings continue to aspire to mediocrity.

Although the scholarly temptation to use this work as a platform to expound upon and probe such cultishly fashionable topics as Is "Lightninging" Correct Participial Usage? Is "Chiropractic" an Adjective or a Ripoff? Is "Raviolum" the Proper Singular? and Would Genetically Modified Professional Wrestlers Still Tend to Shout? was overwhelming, the author managed to subdue his tendencies in that direction.

Interspersed with the serious entries are certain gratuitous ones (which may or may not be parenthetically pronounced), such as "8-Mile Road," "King of Pop," "Flutterby," "LSD," and "S & M," which serve to relieve the intellectual exhaustion generated by the former and, indeed, may even cause a guffaw or two among outlaw members of the Readers' Resistance, elements of the Disunctuous Underground, Eagle Scouts in Gloves and Garter Belts, and others who have salvaged bits and pieces of the excommunicated national Sense of Humor.

Regional utterances, dialects, Cockneyisms, drawls, broken or compound fractures of English, adolescentese, and the slurrings of drunks, pols, jazz musicians of the '60s, and the aged do not fall under the heading of mispronunciation. For instance, when a spineless (but electable) scoundrel utters a sentence such as "The PREZ-dint was GRAYND-standin," he is not mispronouncing the words "president" and "grand-standing" but merely *drawling* his sentence to a conclusion. The same speaker would, however, say "FOR-tay" when "FORT" is correct (one's specialty). When it comes to regional differences, all I really know for sure is that Bostonians think Chicagoans talk "funny," Chicagoans think Virginians talk "funny," and *everyone* agrees that southern Irishmen sound like Swedes.

R. W. Jackson
Highwood Lane

YOU SAY
to · ma · to

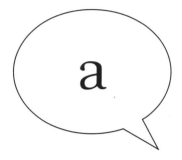

abdomen (AB-duh-mun), *n.* In Americans, the part of the anatomy that speaks loudest for consumerism, according to the CDC (Center for Dyspeptic Citizens) and Dr. Phil Phillups, spokespersonage for the Clinic for the Morbidly Potato-Chipped. *ab-DOUGH-mun,* when going for thirds.

abecedary (A-bih-SEE-duh-re), *n.*, *adj.* Today, "abecedarian" (*a-bih-see-DAIR-e-un*). A person just learning

3

the alphabet, such as a high school sophomore, football coach, or guidance counselor. Both spelling *and* pronunciation are problematic in this case.

aborigine (ab-uh-RIJ-nee), *n.* An indigenous resident with no written language and said to possess crude personal habits and primitive tools with which to work the tourists (as distinguished from rural Republicans, who are subsidized). *ab-uh-RIJ-uh-nee*, nay.

absentee ballot, *phr.* In the USA and Florida, one absent from the count.

absinthe (AB-sinth), *n.* A meaningless catchword invented by a wise man of the coffeehouse persuasion.

academia (AK-uh-DEM-e-uh), *n.* The scholastic community in general, or in particular, Academe (*AK-uh-deem*), the academy where Plato spouted Socratitudes.

academician (uh-kad-uh-MISH-un), *n.* A member of an academy; a true intellectual; one who considers his/her reputation ruined by making the *New York Times* bestseller list. *AK-uh-duh-MISH-un*, on the street.

accessory (ak-SESS-uh-re), *n.* An extra, addition, not included in the base price. For instance, in urban America a man is an accessory *before the fact* of pregnancy but absent as a husband *after the fact* of childbirth, in which case he becomes an *ASS-ess-uh-re*.

acclimate (AK-luh-mate), *v.* To accustom or become accustomed to staleness and failure while withering from age, destitution, Oscar nods, or royalty reports. *uh–KLIH-mit* being currently frozen over.

accoutrement (uh-KOO-truh-munt), *n.* A basic human trapping or supply needed to remain comfortable while waging war, finagling at business, or cheating at sport. *uh-KOO-truh-MAW(N)* is French for "Monsieur G.I., please save our butts (again)."

acumen (uh-KYOO-mun), *n.* Sharpness. A quality mysteriously absent from homogenized twenty-first-century studentry (except in the area of cheating), even though most of their uneducable little heads do top off at a rather nice point. *AK-you-mun*, by the upper declassmen.

a

adamantine (ad-uh-MAN-tin), *adj*. Inflexible; unyielding; fixed; hard as nails; set in concrete; such as Washington's posture toward Havana or Larry King's suspenders. *AD-uh-mun-teen* and *ad-uh-MAN-tine* are set in plastic.

Adolf (AD-awlf). As in Hitler, *Time* magazine's 1939 Man of the Year, an "honor" that has caused a *fuehrer* among the Neville Chamberlains of the world ever since. (And rumor had it that his backhand stank.) *A-dawlf* gets an F.

adult (uh-DULLT), *n*. The prefix of -erous, -erate, -erer, -eress, etc. *ADD-ult* is correctless, on occasion.

advertisement (ad-vur-TIZE-munt), *n*. A solicitation to profligacy; that which put the *mad* in Madison Avenue. *AD-vur-tize-ment* is errorous, but partially salutable. *ad-VURT-iss-munt* has some stature among royal Rhode Islanders.

aeon (E-un, E-ahn), *n*. An age; an eternity; the time reserved for a Los Angelean to drive three blocks; the time it takes a modern Hollywood movie to get to the freaking title; an indefinite period, as in a soccer match or a scorned woman.

Aesop (E-sup), *n*. Fabled Greek moralist, *circa* 620–560 B.C. Led unsuccessful bid to edge out Aeschylus (*E-skuh-lus*) as first name in International Index of Authors. Beloved of future generations and plagiarized accordingly. *S-up* is logical, *A-sup* is legit, and *'sup* is ill.

afferent (A-fuh-runt), *adj*. Of the nerve fibers that carry messages *to* the brain, as distinguished from "affront" (*uh-FRUNT*), or the nerve fibers carrying messages *from* the brain.

agile (AJ-uhl), *adj*. Afflicted with agility; disposed to leaping about and such; nimble of body, numble of mind. Implies vivacity, gyration, noise, or other youthful irritants. *AJ-isle* may be preferred by the British and the Australish.

alleged (uh-LEJD, uh-LEJ-id), *adj*. In the United States of Litigia and the Republic of CYA (Cover Your Ass), an expression even more overused by the grammar-graceless than "no problem" and "it's all good."

alma mater (AL-muh MAH-tur), *n*. Latin for "fostering mother." Designative of an institution of hired learning providing daycare for the intellectually plucky and the sportingly dense. Degree ceremonies are said to be accompanied by overtones of pompous and circumstantial evidence and the awarding of a pigskin. *AL-muh MAT-tur* is popular but ultimately flunks out.

almond (AH-mund), *n*. The fruit of a small tree. There are two types of almond: the "sweet," reserved for tea cakes; and the "bitter," which can be turned into weapons-grade marzipan at a moment's notice. *ALL-mund* is not allowable.

Al Qaeda (awl ki-E-duh), *n*. A patchwork of murderers seeking to liberate busy Western infidels from hot tubs, gas-guzzlers, cruise ships, flash mobs, nose rings, tattoos, triple cheeseburgers, topless shoeshine parlors, teen magazines, Hollywood movies, the Ad Council, charity balls, opium dens, drive-thru gun shops, rap singles, laugh tracks, promising portfolios, and a healthy preoccupation with J.Lo's love life. *al KI-duh* and *al KAY-duh* are acceptable newsmercialese from pundits weaned on Slurpees.

altruist (AL-troo-ist), *n*. One of the misanthropically impaired. *AWL-troo-ist* lives in the vicinity of error-hood.

aluminum (uh-LOO-mih-numb), *n*. A base metal out of which the ear of youth is constructed in the absence of good tin. The Brits and southern Hoosiers prefer *AL-yoo-MIN-e-um*.

Alzheimer (AWLTS-hi-mur), **Alois** (1864–1915). German physician credited with describing "senior dementia." Pronunciation ranges from *OLD-ti-mur*, for milder forms of the disease characterized, for instance, by forgetting where you put the keys to the White House or showing up naked to render the majority opinion, to *AILZ-hi-mur* for more severe forms of the malady.

ambidextrous (am-buh-DEK-strus), *adj*. Able to deal off the bottom with either hand.

amen (A-MEN), *interj.* An expression of approval. A rather key word in the Sunday sermon, serving as a stimulus for male members of the congregation to wake up and go home. *AH-MEN* is more popular in some pews than in others.

Amherst (AM-urst), *n.* Massachusetts town high on the New England Transcendental list. Among local touriosities is the preserved house that Emily was a little dickens in. *AM-hurst* seems to be the preference of legal aliens and triple-dipping pensioners banished from Branson.

Amish (AHM-ish), *n.* After Jacob Amman. Mennonites who moved to America to get away from worldly things. (It is not known which travel guide was consulted.) *AIM-ish* and *A-mish* are the one-horse pronunciations.

anathema (uh-NATH-uh-muh), *n.* Some damned thing or person, cursed, banned, or banished by ecclesiastical authority or, worse, Bill O'Reilly. Currently nominatively predicated, as in "the word 'gambling' is anathema to casino spokespersons and gaming commission board members" or "Tailoring, grooming, hygiene, courtesy, manners, and self-control are anathema to professional athletes." The word "draft" is anathema to U.S. "commanders" in Iraq. *AN-uh-THEE-muh*, nah.

anchor (ANG-kur), *n*. A dead weight employed to keep a craft from going anywhere, or to prevent a derelict from drifting from channel to channel. Mispronunciation is an option. Pretty Fox-y, huh?

anchovy (AN-cho-vee), *n*. The shrimp of the herring family; commonly designed into a pizza one wishes not to share. *an-CHO-vee* is incorrect, unless in verse.

androgynous (an-DRAH-juh-nus), *adj*. Ambisextrous.

anecdote (AN-ik-dote), *n*. A boring narrative beloved by dolts who dote on making a short story long. Ingenuously confused with "antidote" by those fortunate enough to have avoided the company of a teller of anecdotes.

angst (AHNGST), *n*. 1. Ecstatic agony; the Woody Allen syndrome; what Boomers and Xers are supposed to be full of, among other things. 2. The calm before the Sturm und Drang, that is, before your 401(k) goes south. *AINGST* borders on the new erotic.

angstrom (AING-strum), *n.* One hundred-millionth of a centimeter, or the distance rapper 50 Cent is able to carry a tune. *ONG-strum* is preferred by hard rockers.

Antarctica (ant-ARK-tih-kuh), *n.* The "South Pole." A pristine land lacking a population of natives to slaughter over mineral rights. Also, the region of the globe where the Social Security Endowment Fund is said to currently reside. *ant-ART-ih-kuh* is slowly freezing out the former.

antibiotic (an-te-by-AH-tik), *n.* Med-sin, according to Mary Baker Eddy. *AN-tuh-by-AH-tik,* popularly.

Antigua (an-TEE-guh, an-TEE-gwuh), *n.* West Indies island and favorite cruiser port of the portly.

antiperspirant (ANN-ty-PURR-spur-unt), *n.* A preparation used to keep the armpits dry while telling a lie. *ANN-tee* isn't.

apartheid (uh-PAHR-tayt, uh-PAHR-tight), *n.* The Republic of South Africa's version of racial segregation, interdicted by Nelson Mandela. Today, racial relations in South Africa are said to be just as amicable as they are in Mississippi or Orange County.

apostrophe (uh-PAHS-truh-fee), *n.* A mark of punctuation missing, along with adverbs and articles, from general correspondence, casual conversation, and/or business signage composed by post-1975 mortarboarders.

apothegm (AP-uh-them), *n.* A short, witty saying, modern authors of which have seen fit to economize upon even further by dispensing with the wit. *AP-oh-tem* is incorrect.

Appalachia (APP-uh-LAY-chuh), *n.* A scenic area extending south from querulous Quebec to northern Alabama, where thoughts of secession yet linger, where tarts who write mash notes to incarcerated serial murderers are bred, and where English subtitles are required for day-to-day communications, especially in the Alabama part. Heady social rituals include the "coming of age" party, with the presenting of assorted lollipops and a list of eligible cousins. *app-uh-LAY-shuh* is fine only if you're a-namin' or appealin', hoss.

apparatus (AP-uh-RAH-tus), *n*. Mechanism; complication; implements. Implies a harmonious dysfunction such as in a "political machine," an intelligence community, or a nuclear family.

applicable (AP-li-kuh-b'l), *adj*. That can be advantageously applied, suitably contrived, conveniently quoted out of context, profitably appointed, untraceably plagiarized, etc. *uh-PLIK-uh-b'l* is said to be the darling of the Biden/Reagan School of Advised Amnesia.

apricot (A-pruh-kaht), *n*. A small yellowish-orange tree fruit, edible dried or as jam, to which mystical properties of longevity are attributed, mostly by petulant hypochondriacs who will pass on in spite of it. *AP-ri-kot* being the alternate.

a priori (AY-pry-OR-i, AH-pre-OR-e) An expression appearing in most dictionaries directly after "April Fools' Day." A method of reasoning based on Sherlock

Holmes or John Grisham rather than Danielle Steele or Harold Robbins, whose works are said to be covered under "a posteriori." *AH-pre-OR-I* for those left to repeat Logic 101 and viewers who preferred *Pantomime Quiz* to *Firing Line*.

Arab (AHR-ub), *n*. A Semite from the Arabian peninsula; a Mohammedan. *AIR-ub* is considered acceptable; *AY-rab* is American dialectical pronunciation.

armada (ar-MAH-duh), *n*. From the Spanish for "armed force." Historically, a fleet of Spanish warships (called "the Invincible Armada") that was vinced by the English Navy in 1588—reportedly, the year of the debut of *The Price Is Right*. *ar-MAY-duh* is the leaky version.

a

ars longa, vita brevis (AHRZ LAWN-guh, WEE-tuh BRE-wis), *phr*. Latin for "Art is long, life is short"—as quoted from Hippocrates, Seneca, Browning, Kurt Cobain. (Browning uttered it in English, apparently in a weak moment.)

arthritis (ahr-THRY-tus), *n*. Inflammation of a joint, said to be curable by going to Arizona, which in turn is said to be curable by going to San Francisco, Belize, Toronto, Manhattan, etc. *AHR-thur-I-tus* is a familiar groan.

ascetic (uh-SET-ik), *n.* One who lives a life of isolation, abstinence, and contemplation for various reasons having to do with spiritual enlightenment. In the USA, enlightenment comes with either federal, state, or county oversight at no extra charge, although, according to the grapevine, "abstinence" has seen some upgrades. *uh-SEAT-ik*, incorrectionally.

asexual (ay-SEK-shoe-ul), *adj.* Sexless; devoid of sexuality; prone to being caught with one's pants up.

ask (ASK), *v.* To invite obfuscation, prevarication, complication, justification, and cover-up. Not a serious pronunciation problem, except among the regionally tongue-tied and the phonemically disabled, who have been known to pronounce it as *AKS*.

asphalt (ASS-fawlt), *n.* Commonly, a federal concoction consisting of one part evaporated petroleum, two parts sand, and three parts pork—steamrolled by

a

the highwaymen on the Hill. *ASH-fawlt* is the preference of the *GROWSH-ry* crowd.

aspirant (uh-SPY-runt), *n*. One having played into the hands of the Horatio Alger conspiracy; a barefoot reality-show contestant seeking out disappointment rather than waiting for it to come naturally. *ASS-pur-unt* is slightly overmedicated.

assize (uh-SIZE), *n*. In the U.K., a court session or a decree stemming from it, with regard to criminal or civil cases. The plaintiff frequently pronounces it incorrectly.

a

assuage (uh-SWAYJ), *v.t.* To lessen the effect or pain of. To calm, for instance, a victim of express-lane rage or anyone caught in the vortex of psycho Boston drivers or pension-fund meltdown; to console those having heard that the reality show *Surviving for a Year Eating Only Raw Ostrich Gizzards and Drinking Wombat Pee in Uptown Calcutta* has been canceled; to allay the frustration and thoughts of justifiable homicide in those having to deal on a regular basis with colleagues whose vocabularies are limited to "no problem," "VIN number," "PIN number," "ATM machine," "what goes around comes around," "personal friend of mine," "in *my* day . . . ," "that's why there's a food chain," "play it again, Sam," "no skin off my nose," and/or "if I don't see you before the holiday, have a happy . . ." (what if he *does* see you before the holiday?); to comfort those having attended the funeral of the adverb. *uh-SEWAGE* is incorrect, but not by much.

asterisk (ASS-tur-isk), *n*. A star-shaped symbol (*) indicating a footnote, change, or omission in an original text, etc. Recently, asterisks have been found clinging in rather large numbers to professional sports records set by "well-tested" and important players. The Major League Select Ethics Committee, however, is said to be aware of the situation and, in order to preserve the sanctity of "the game" and make sure that the nation's youths are not adversely influenced by false allegations against "the game," will be conducting an internal investigation, possibly as soon as the season after next. *AZ-tur-ik* and *ASS-tur-ik* are common, merely because of sloppiness in *educanunciation*.

atavism (ATT-uh-viz'm), *n.* 1. A reversion, or a throwback taking the form of, for instance, a pensioner with a rotary-dial cell phone or a modern author relying on a mechanical typewriter. 2. Something that *should* be thrown back, such as a Ford Thunderbird or a Mötley Crüe.

atheist (AY-thee-ist), *n.* A member of a non-prophet organization. One who does not believe in revealed religion but might be an Agnostic (questions the existence of God, Heaven, Hell, taste among hip-hoppers, and sobriety among judges), a Deist (believes in God but not in revealed religion, the immanence of God, or that *Fight Club* and *Red Dragon* have any redeeming social, artistic, or literary value), a Free-thinker (rejects formal religion as incompatible with reason but secretly prays that the herpes will go away), or an Infidel (believes that all religions embody peace and justice after they gain power through intimidation, terrorism, and murder), and agrees with the hypothesis that Grammar and Spell Check are programs designed by boobs. *ay-THEE-ist* by those who believe that loafers without socks isn't silly.

atherosclerosis (AH-thur-o-skluh-ROE-sus), *n.* A word frequently confused with "arteriosclerosis," but slightly more so outside the medical profession than in. The former being a condition where an internist would first pimp for the pharmacist rather than suggest a low-cholesterol diet.

Atlantis (at-LAN-tis), *n.* An halluci nation.

audiophile (AW-de-o-file), *n.* One appreciative of divertimentos, partitas, passacaglias, motets, oratorios, and the Sex Pistols merely through a two-inch speaker or two; as distinguished from *AW-de-o-PHOOLZ,* who are unable to (dis)function unaccompanied by blare.

augury (AWE-gyuh-re), *n.* The ancient and priestly science of predicting political trends based on omens. It has been downgraded in the modern world, which is left merely with the New Hampshire Primary. *AWE-guh-re* will pass in Iowa.

automaton (aw-TAH-muh-tahn), *n.* A robotnik; an entry-level zombie. That which functions automatically, mechanically, or woodenly, or appears to be battery-operated, such as a teenager, an airport security guard, or Condi Rice. This is not meant to reflect negatively on the "Automat," a pioneer purveyor of fast–food in New York City around the time of Boss Tweed, or when Julia Child—God love her—was still a soprano. *AW-TOE-mat-tun* is warmed over.

autopsy (AWE-top-see), *n*. An outpatient procedure conducted in order to determine the exact cause of homicide. (Natural homicides are exempt.)

auxiliary (awg-ZIL-yuh-ree), *adj*. Backing-up or supplementing the main source of, for instance, corruption, drug-running, gun-running, rigged elections, mind control, surveillance, scandal, secret police, and other 1984 entitlements for 2020 America.

aviatrix (AY-ve-AY-triks), *n*. A fine word for a female aviator, especially one who does tricks (stunts). *A-ve-uh-triks* doesn't fly.

avoirdupois (ah-vur-duh-POIZ), *n*. French for "to have goods." An Anglo-American system of weights based on an ounce of 16 drams:

16 drams = 1 ounce
16 ounces = 1 pound
2000 pounds = 1 ton
16 tons = Tennessee Ernie Ford, Michael Moore (or less), Brando's coffin, Oprah in an off-diet season while on the outs with what's his name (Stedman?).

AV-ur-DOO-pwar is incorrect, unless you owe your doopwar to the company store.

a

badminton (BAD-min-tun), *n*. A desperately silly game invented in the Orient and having gravitated naturally to the duchies of Victorian England, along with other abominations such as curry. It was taken seriously by Americans during the reign of Herbert Hoover. *BAD-mitten* is just as worse.

Baldwin bluefin, *n*. A piano tuna.

banal (BAY-n'l), *adj*. Commonplace, drab, trite; so devoid of charm and substance as to be worthy of a motivational speaker, a schlock jock, an apologist, a sloganeer, an episode of *The Apprentice*, or a California sherry. *buh-NAL*, according to the grapevine.

basil (BAZ'l), *n*. Name of an herb so tasty as to have been canonized by the Cappadocians after the fifth century A.D. A feast is held in its honor on June 14. (Its traditional *panamour* is Rosemary.) *BAY-zul* is unsavory to the point of being popular. What *would* the Rathbones think!

bas-relief (baa-rih-LEEF), *n*. Contrary to what you're thinking, this has nothing to do with the sexual preference of terrorists, alarmists, grifters, road-ragers, book-burners, genocidos, anti-Semites, or wire frauds. It is a wall sculpture with depth, or projection, if you will. *BAA-rih-leef* is acceptable.

beaux-arts (bo-ZAR), *n*. French for "fine arts." Pronounced as *BO-zartz* by climbers, including the bozos in the arts.

Beelzebub (be-EL-ze-bub), *n.* Hebrew for "ba'alzevuv" ("lord of flies"). An incarnation of Satan said to preside over attorneys' zippers; in Milton's *Paradise Lost,* a fallen angel with certain political qualities as might become all public *serpents*. *BEEL-ze-bub*, erroneously.

behemoth (bih-HE-muth), *n.* An extraordinarily large beast or thing. A word now just coming into its own in the wake of the fast-food ship of the States and its attendant super-sized citizenry. This word has received recent updating in the form of "bih-SHE-muth," according to picket signs at the recent Ms. Musclemania pageant in Cicero, IL, the editors of *La Petit Fem* magazine, and apprentice videographers embedded with directors of the smash-hit reality show *Girls Gone Wide*.

Bela (BAY-luh), *n.* Given name, mostly of Hungarian men: Bela Lugosi (actor), Bela Karoli (trainer), Bela Bartok (cacophonist), to name the popular ones. *BELL-uh* is common to the point of insult, with all apologies to Ms. Abzug (Bella).

"Belgium Waffle" (BELL-jun), *n.* Why can't restaurants get this right? Are they too busy undersalting the sauces, overcooking (and misspelling) omelets, ignoring the greasy salt and pepper shakers, selling pork as "veal," downgrading the wine list, prosecuting grandmothers for stealing everything but the tablecloths? What is it? It's *Belgian* Waffle, is what it is.

belles-lettres (bell-LET-ruh). French for "beautiful letters." Fine literature, sharp criticism, charming word books, etc., as opposed to training manuals, guest columns, celebrity weeklies. A phrase commonly heard expressed in hushed tones by postulants selectively admitted to the Thomas Pynchon Sighting Society on the Upper West Side of Manhattan.

Bernstein (BURN-stine), **Leonard** (1918–1990). Maestro. American conductor, composer, soloist, author, teacher, lecturer, mentor, student, impresario, classicist, popularist, West Side Storian. *BURN-steen*, forgivably.

bestiality (bess-che-AH-luh-te), *n.* From "bestial" (*BES-chul*)—beastly, brutal, coarse, businesslike, etc. Media-approved pronunciation is *BEAST-e-AL-ih-te*, of *coarse*, for the hunkerly masses. They ought to know.

bettor (BET-tur), *n*. A loser with money. *BET-tor*, not.

bibulous (BIB-yuh-lus), *adj*. Not averse to an olive spiritually awash.

bicyclist (BI-sih-klist), *n*. A pedalophile.

billion, *n*. After taxes, penalties, restitution, fines, and a suspended sentence, what a corporate criminal is left with.

Bin Laden (bin-LAH-dun), **Osama** (o-SAH-muh) (1957–   ). The Pol Pot of Islam, without the charisma. Itinerant murderer and aspiring Luddite; refuses to upgrade into seventeenth century; reputedly has forty-five offspring from seven wives, three daughters, and a goat. And he doesn't even play golf! Spelling and pronunciation of this name are from the same school as that of Mohamar Kqhadahffilthy.

Bizet (be-ZAY), **Georges** (ZHORZH) (1838–1875). French composer most notably of "listenable" opera *Carmen*. Left note in his will to the effect that should the piece ever be mounted as a "suite" or "fantasy" (opera without words), the perpetrators were to be seized-up and flogged to the bone under the Arc de Triomphe. Pronounced as *bih-ZET* by cell-phonies and library talkers.

blackguard (BLAH-gurd), *n*. A hoodlum; a milder sort of wretch than, say, an assassin, a terrorist, or a Little League dad. *BLAK-gahrd* is acceptable around the diamond.

blog (BLAHg), *v*. To BLAH BLAH BLAH BLAH BLAH.

"B" movie, *n*. Footage wherein one is left to root for the villain (monster, Mothra, screenwriter, etc.) and then, more vigorously, for The End.

boatswain (BO-s'n), *n*. A ship's officer in charge of the deck crew. The coxswain (*KAHK-s'n*) steers the craft and/or calls the cadence of rowers, who are usually located downwind from the poop (*POOP*). Can you handle the punch line for this one yourself?

bona fide (BO-nuh-fide), *adj.* Latin for "in good faith." Without fraud, malice, or deceit—until gaining access to the high-speed Internet.

boor (BOOR), *n.* An ill-mannered person (usually male), with tin ear and mouth to match, who may appear rather homely, badly groomed, inbred, and smelly around the meth pile, snuff dip, ammo dump, camo camp, etc.

boughten (BAW-tuhn). Past imperfect participle of "buy." Must be used with "had," as in "He had forgotten that he had boughten the edible undies for his secretary until the bill had showed up on his wife's Visa statement."

bouquet, *n.* Thanks to Pat Boone and "April Love," this word is pronounced almost exclusively as *boo-KAY:* an aroma. Boone, of course, meant *bo-KAY:* a flower arrangement. But what do you expect from a guy who wears white bucks and a garter belt! (Stacked heels would be much more appropriate.)

boutonniere (boot'n-EER), *n.* A flower worn on the lapel by mourners at a wedding or by captains of indifferent service.

bovine (BO-vine), *adj.* Latin for "ox-like" or "lineman-like." Hence of a stalwart beast, the male of which species is said to encourage the stealthy input of hormone enhancements, giving aid and comfort to the bacteriologist who, in light of the international beefs about mad cow disease, is prone to suspect all the usual roundups. *BO-veen* is hamburger. Bovinity is also at the bottom of those whose fecal output is discursively discussed. It's a moo-ed point.

bowdlerize (BODE-luh-rize), *v.* After Dr. Thomas Bowdler, nineteenth-century anti-first-amend-menter. To bowdlerize means to remove "tasteless" passages from literature and put them on TV, where they will be appreciated.

Bowdoin (BO-d'n), *n.* Coeducational institution at Brunswick, Maine, named for James Bowdoin (1726–1790), conservative political figure and suppressor of Shay's (farmers') Rebellion (1786–87), in which Willie Nelson insists he played no part. Courses include such Maine-stays as Ethnological Positivism and Sensitivity Proclivity. Faculty known for tenure tantrums. *BO-doyn* and *bo-DOYEN* are accepted misvoicednesses.

Bowie (BO-e), **Colonel James** (1799–1836). Texas hero who died at the Alamo. As distinguished from David, who *dyes* otherwise. The former is credited with the invention of the Bowie knife, the latter the invention of federally prosecutable hair. *BOO-e* is phooey.

Brisbane (BRIZ-bun), *n.* An Australian city where talk is sheep; the capital of Queensland (*KWEENZ-lund*), a large metropolis on the east coast, north of Sydney. *BRIZ-bane* is okay in America, where students are taught that the Austro-Hungarian Empire was founded by Captain Cook in 1770 as a penile colony for Shropshire child molesters.

brothel (BRAH-thul), *n.* A little shop of whores. From the French "brethen," meaning "to waste away" . . . especially after you have visited a brothel. *BRU-thul* is venerably immaterial to us.

Buckingham (BUCK-ing-um), *n.* Royal residence, after the Duke of Buckingham. Site of Queen Elizabeth's Golden Jubilee & Ribs Festival (winter 2005). Also, reputed future site of first annual Arnold vs. Camilla Battle of the Thighs contest. *BUCK-ing-ham,* for the Yanks.

Budapest (BOO-duh-pest), *n.* Hungarian metropolis sometimes referred to as the "Paris of the Danube," as Rio is called the "Paris of the South," Beirut the "Paris of the Mideast," and Detroit the "Plaster of Paris." *YO-nuh-poat ke-vah-NOOK!*

buffet (buh-FAY), *n.* Popularly, a trough catering to more self-servers than a pack of PACs or a sewer full of sociopaths. Cafeteria cousin- and "buffet grandmother"-approved.

buoy (BOO-e), *n.* An anchored float, warning of shoals, shallows, tourists, etc. *v.t.* To keep afloat artificially until the feds catch on.

business (BIZ-nus, BIZ-nis), *n.* Occupationness; flimflamness. No one in the Age of Progress, with the possible exception of those in the cheap seats at a Jeff Foxworthy show, would pronounce this as *BID-nis*. Of course, every day at eBay it's *bidness* as usual.

b

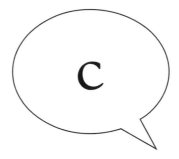

cabal (kuh-BAL), *n.* A plot woven with intrigues that studio executives and rewrite men regularly dilute. See "junta."

Cabala (kuh-BAH-luh), *n.* A system of mystical interpretation of the Scriptures—as if they needed it.

cabana (kuh-BAHN-yuh), *n.* A hut, cottage, or small Mexican beach pavilion invested with overtones of

Brad & Jen, and stocked with designer water and a higher quality of sand fly than your common bungalow. *kuh-BAN-uh* is okay if you can copa with it.

cache (KASH), *n*. A place with something to hide. A word bandied about peace-loving republics and parliamentary democracies to describe an imaginary stockpile of arms or weapons of mass destruction prior to the preemptive invasion and the premature victory crowing.

cachet (KASH-ay, ka-SHAY), *n*. A seal of approval; a seal indicating authenticity or prestige, an undetectable forgery, etc. Also a popular kind of capsule containing sports "medicine."

cadaver (kuh-DA-vur), *n*. A working stiff; remains to be seen. *kuh-DAY-vur* and *KAD-uh-vur* are dead wrong, but the author biers no anatomosity toward them.

cadmium (KAD-me-um), *n*. A metallic chemical element. Ingredient of nuclear reactor shields, rechargeable batteries, and chewing tobacco (yum). *KAD-e-um* is the going rate among the trite and true, even among Cal Techies, alas.

caduceus (kuh-DOO-se-us), *n*. A winged staff with two serpents wound about it, carried by Mercury. Currently a symbol of the medical profession, a number of whose serpents are carried by Mercedes. *kuh-DOO-sis* is a don't.

caliph (KAY-luf), *n*. The head of a Mecca-nized force.

Camaro (cuh-MAIR-o), *n*. A marque of Chevydom. According to undisclosable sources, the Generalissimos of General Motors predicted that the rabble of American car buyers would invariably pronounce it as kuh-MAHR-o. The slogan was to be "Camaro, Car of Tomorrow." GM brass also predicted that Japanese automakers would *not* kick Detroit butt in the '70s and '80s.

candidate (KAN-duh-dayt), *n*. One who runs, usually with good reason. An impenitent custodian of the ringing cliché and the hollow promise. One possessed of no marketable skills and generally unemployable. *KAN-dih-dit* is correct only among the inmates.

cantilever (KAN-tuh-lee-vur), *n*. A bracket-shaped support for an architectural wonder, popular in mud-slide areas. *kan-tuh-LEE-vur* can't deliver.

caoutchouc (KAOOH-chook), *n*. The organic name for common rubber, the chief constituent of the human neck, *kow-CHOOHK* being the alternative.

capsaicin (kap-SAY-uh-sun), *n*. A phenolic amide lending inspiration to certain members of the pepper family. *KAP-suh-sin* and *kap-SAY-sin* are less cool.

carbine (KAHR-byne), *n*. A rifle whose cartridges sit closer to the end of the barrel. In the late 1870s, U.S. cavalrymen carried *single-shot* carbines against the hostiles' Winchester repeaters, a situation that, according to an Army memo of the time, could result in "an occasional compromise of mounted forces, except in the Little Bighorn Command." *KAHR-bean* is less than M-1, A-1.

Caribbean (kair-uh-BEE-un), *adj*. Of the Caribs or Caribals, natives of the southern West Indies who, contrary to reports of their viciousness, regularly had missionaries over for dinner. *n.* A sea lane strewn with retirees. *kuh-RIB-e-un*, cruiserwise.

carpe diem (KAHR-peh-DEE-em). Latin for "seize the day," i.e., make the most of your opportunities despite your inveterate sloth, your clandestine affair with opiates, and your fascination with this eminently quotable tome. Any other pronunciation ought be swept under the carpe.

caveat (KAH-ve-at), *n.* An admonition or warning. Latin for "let him beware." Popular extensions are: caveat emptor (let the buyer beware), caveat priestor (let the altar boy beware), and caveat senator (let the taxpayer beware). *KAV-e-at* and *KAH-ve-aht* are less correct.

Cedric (SED-rik). Celtic for "war chief." A masculine name, at least south of the twentieth century or east of Hollywood. *SEED-rik* grows wild.

cellulite (SELL-yuh-lyte), *n.* Subcutaneous tissue at the bottom of the dieting craze. *SELL-yuh-leet*, optionally.

C

cement (sih-MENT), *n*. A mixture of powdered lime, clay, and water. For *SEE-ment*, add a clod.

censure (SEN-shur), *v*. To apprise a professional of the public's disgust with him. *n*. The blame game. An exercise in discipline as far removed from punishment as bacon is from a synagogue; used principally in a judicial, political, or ecclesiastical sense. Censure does not go beyond finger-pointing, lest the finger pointers' fingers be found deeper in the same till, cookie jar, or choirboy.

cerebral (suh-REE-brul), *adj*. Of or pertaining to the brain. The brain is housed in a chamber called the "cranium," frequently noted for its bone-headedness and affinity for air. *SAIR-ub-brul* is acceptable when used before "palsy."

chaise longue (SHAYZ-LONG), *n*. A large, supportive chair, not unlike the one in which a dentist carries out terrorist-like activities. *CHASE LOUNJ*, after the chase.

chamois (SHAH-me), *n.* Small Eurasian antelope. Trophies displayed in auto parts stores. *sham-WAH* is discorrect, except at the *Concours d' Elegance* and the *Pissoir d' Joe's Bar.*

chancellor (CHAN-suh-lur), *n.* A university official subordinate to the highest-ranking official, that is, the football coach. *CHAN-suh-lor,* secondarily.

chantey (SHAN-tee), *n.* A sailor's working song, once said by Captain Bligh to be indicative of pre-minstrel syndrome.

chassis (SHA-see), *n.* A frame or framework, not necessarily including parts. Slang: a woman's body, especially parts, some of which not necessarily being the manufacturer's original. *CHAS-ee,* by the unclassy.

chaste (CHAYST), *adj.* Unchased. *CHAST* and *CHAYST-ih-ty* are incorrect.

Cheops (KE-ops), *pn.* Greek name for Khufu (*KOO-foo*), son of Snafu and king of ancient Egypt. Cheops founded the Fourth Dynasty and built the great pyramid at Gizeh in 3,000 B.C. (Before Concrete). *CHEE-ops* is incorrect.

Chicago (shuh-KAH-go), *n.* Major U.S. city in the northern midlands; home, at one time or another, to such diverse personalities as Carl Sandburg, Richard Daley, and Abbie Hoffman. *chik-AH-go*, on Rush street. (The movie *Chicago*, incidentally, was filmed in Canada, where they have police.)

Circe (SUR-see), *n.* An evil goddess; a bad-ass babe who changed men into beasts and women into housewives.

civilization (SIV-uh-luh-ZAY-shun), *n.* The loosely worn garments of savagery.

Chevy Chase (CHEV-ee CHASE), *n.* Name of fifteenth-century English ballad about the Percy and Douglas families, the Hatfields and McCoys of Great Britain. Also the name of a Maryland village and a tall comedian. *SHEV-ee* is no good; just ask a Honda dealer.

Chile (CHIL-ee), *n.* A California-suffering-from-anorexia-shaped country in South America. *CHEE-leh* or *CHEE-lay* in North American Newsspeak.

chimera (kuh-MIR-uh), *n.* A fire-breathing monster with the head of a lion, the tail of a serpent, and the body of an SUV.

Cimmeria (suh-MIR-e-uh), *n.* A land described by Homer as a place being in a perpetual fog, extending from Venice along the Pacific Coast Highway through Santa Monica and Malibu and ending at San Simeon.

clapboard (KLA-burd), *n.* A material said to be pre-eminent in the construction of certain kinds of houses. As in "You're gonorrheally like it here, sailor."

Clio (KLY-o), *n.* The mythological muse of history. One of nine inspirational Greek goddesses of the arts and sciences, whose influence is seen in the works of almost an equal number of Western artists and thinkers since Pericles. *KLEE-o* is no-no.

C

clique (KLEEK), *n.* A sect-like circle of persons with mutually stuffy interests. Elitism for the masses; bargain-basement clubbiness. *KLIK*, to the in-crowd; *KLIK-ee*, to righteous reviewers.

Codeine (KO-deen), *n.* A démodé narcotic preferred by clean-shaven addicts with regular haircuts.

coelacanth (SEE-luh-kanth), *n.* Lungfish. A "living fossil" predating Senator Byrd.

Coetzee (kut-ZEE-uh), **John Michael (J. M.)** (1940–). Brilliant South African novelist. Champion of the underdog; friend to animals; promising career cut short by Nobel Prize. *KOAT-see* to residents of the Republic of Mediastan and the Drivelian Archipelago, incredulous at the annual snubbing of Philip Roth.

Cockburn (KO-burn), *n.* Surname, usually. Also the name of a line of Portuguese port wines. *KAHK-burn* is okay if you're into cuckoldry.

Colin (KAH-lun). Masculine (at this writing) given name. No one in his right mind would pronounce this as *KO-lun*, as in a part of an intestine or a mark of punctuation, would he?

comfortable (KUMF-tur-bull), *adj.* Secure in the knowledge of a neighbor's bankruptcy, a sister's BMW repo, a celebrity's addictions, a priest's defrockment, an ex-spouse's STD, a cousin's ouster from the will, etc. *KUM-furt-a-bull* being anything but.

compote (KAHM-pote), *n.* An array of stewed fruits, as distinguished from compost (or not). *kahm-POE-tee*, no, although Truman would've loved it.

Conan Doyle (KO-nun DOYL) (1859–1930). A published Arthur.

concert (KAHN-surt), *n.* A word forced into quotation marks against its will and before its time. A (con)junction of players, recently broadened to include the imperfectly tuxedofied if not thoroughly 'toxified.

concierge (kon-SYERZH), *n.* A procurement officer and logistical support overseer of distinguished hostelries and upscale apartment buildings. (Michelin reports that clients by the name of John receive the best service.)

concubine (KAHNG-kew-byne), *n.* A woman whose choice of a mate has been, to some extent, delimited and who, in fact, may appear somewhat reluctant at nuptials, except in the seraglios of Salt Lake City, where variety is the spice of *wife*.

condescend (con-di-SEND), *v.i.* To con while descending from on High, the Right and Left wings flapping as one. Condescenders can be identified by their noses, which cruise at twelve thousand feet, and typically are those having been successfully inbred from the "A" list of schmucks, inheritors, scoundrels, sportsmen, clubmen, junior leaguers, and disappointed mothers-in-law. Some are known to be rather irresistibly drawn to the "I'd rather be . . ." bumper sticker, while *all* remain perplexed at the stench of their stool.

congeries (KAHN-juh-reez), *n.* A pile or heap of disparate objects haphazardly thrown together. In other words, a freshmen congressman orientation. Or, as Thomas Jefferson would like to have put it: "The Capitole, congested by a coterie of concupiscent craqpotts and conniving congeriesmen."

conjugal (KAHN-ji-gul), *adj*. Of or relating to matrimoany.

Connecticut (kuh-NEH-tih-kuht), *n*. One of the thirteen original States of the United States. Significant as home to naval base at Groton (GRAH-t'n), whose Rooseveltian motto is "Speak softly and carry an undetectable nuclear-powered submarine fleet." The state is also famed as home base of the brilliant inventor of back-up lights for motorcycles, as well as the critically acclaimed and wildly bestselling author of *The Five People You Meet in New Haven*, the names of whom have temporarily slipped the author's word processor.

conquistadors (kahn-KWIS-tuh-doors), *n*. Prepetroleum rapists and gold diggers in the New World. Led impressionable Native Americans to believe that they were European talent scouts searching for the fabled Seven Cities of Sybil Shepherd. From the way the conquistadors were dressed, the natives tended to believe them. *kahn-KEES-tuh-doors* is popular among enlightened rapaciousists.

controversial (kahn-truh-VUR-shul), *adj.* Awkward; debatable; delicate; questionable; such as the questionability of the integrity of pure-as-the-driven-snow-job bankers and credit card companies or the moral/ethical debate of whether or not to remove the feeding tube from unfortunate individuals who are in fact brain-dead, such as Terri Schiavo (*she-AH-vo*) or Bobby Fischer. *kahn-truh-VUR-see-ul* is gaining on the outside, even among those of the Subtractive School of Syllabification.

conundra (kuh-NUN-druh), *n.* Plural of "conundrum." Things that are difficult to assess, or account for, or questions that are tough to answer, such as: "Does the prime number pairs mysterium cause unexplained sightings of The Captain and Tenille?" "Could Bigfoot be fitted at Nordstrom's?" "Should the U.S. Air Force Academy be included in *Screw* magazine's list of the 69 most desirable destinations?" "Are the crop circles in Shea Stadium and Qualcomm Field related?" Etc.

Copenhagen (ko-pun-HAY-gun), *n.* The capital of Denmark. Imports include metals, fuels, and *George* Jorgensen. Exports include pharmaceuticals, machinery, and *Christine* Jorgensen. *KO-pun-hah-gen* and *KO-pun-hay-gun* are incorrect.

cordial (KAWR-jul), *n.* A high-carb inebriant for those who prefer a toothache and a hangover to just a hangover.

cornet (kor-NET), *n.* A musical instrument resembling a trumpet. Toss in another "o" and you've got "coronet" a headdress of flowers (*KOR-uh-NET*), formerly worn by a lady superior to a strumpet. Both invariably mispronounced.

cosmology / cosmetology, *n.* "Wanted: Cosmologist for upscale salon in Beverly Hills. Pay equal to knowledge of stars."

coterie (KO-tuh-ree), *n.* Originally, a feudal organization of landholding peasants. Now, *any* organization of peasants: lodge, fraternity, club, clan, clique, sect, circle, group, etc.

C

coup d'etat (koo-day-TAH), *phr.* French for "stroke of state." When the State suffers a stroke its speech will slur, its vision will blur, and it will experience paralysis on the Right. It will also allow rebel forces to take over radio and television broadcasting, thank God!

coupon (KOO-pahn), *n.* Suburbanese for "How long can I block the 'Eight Items or Less' line with fifteen items or more, six of which aren't bar-coded? And will the old fart behind me get off on 'justifiable homicide'?"

couscous (KOOS-KOOS), *n.* A gastronomical blank canvas. Synonyms: pastapasta, ricerice, tatertater.

Cowan (KOW-un). A long-suffering surname, invariably pronounced as *KO-un.*

coyote (KI-oat), *n.* The coyote (*Canis latrans*) is a small wolf about six times the size of the miniature poodle (*Canis yappus*), upon which it likes to dine in the absence of rabbits and two-year-olds. *ki-OH-tee* is the pronunciation of endearment.

creek (KREEK), *n*. A stream not as shallow as a babbling brook or a campaign promise, but deep enough to drown a pedophile, rapist, non-voter, jury-dodger, or CEO. *KRICK* is favored by the hick.

crème de cacao (KREEM duh KO-ko), *n*. French for "cream of cocoa." A sweet chocolate liqueur. Parisians, Villagers, and some members of the alternative retirement underground are said to, on occasion, even apply it *in*ternally.

crème de la crème (KREM duh lah KREM), *n*. French for "cream of the cream." The absolute best of something traditionally overrated.

Crete (KREET), *n*. Island in the Eastern Mediterranean held by Greece until invasion by Princess Cruise Lines in 1972. Native lifestyle said to be similar to that of Southern California Cretins. *KRAYT* is wrong.

crises (KRY-seez), *n*. The plural of "crise," a mediastical favorite the meaning of which will have been lost to perpetuital yawns.

Cro-Magnon (kro-MAG-nun), *n.* A prehysteric man similar to modern man but whose skeletal remains suggested *two* ears and only *one* mouth.

crone (KROHN), *n.* An old, old, old, old woman. But not as old as greed, corruption, ignorance, poverty, selfishness, vanity, the campaign cliché, the political platitude, or the Queen's hat. A "crony" (*KRO-nee*) is a person appointed to fill the seat of an office with no requirement for any filling in his head. Cronyism is now practiced in America but was first perfected in France.

cryonics (kry-AH-niks), *n.* Method for storing human remains that retains most of the flavor.

culinary (KULL-uh-ner-ee), *adj.* From the Latin "culinarius," meaning "kitchen." As the great Roman orator and kitchenator Emerilius Bammus once mused, "Two things, only, occupied our minds just before the fall of our beloved Rome: food and entertainment." "Culinary" remains a most abused word both pronunciation- and gastronomy-wise. "Kilarney," now, is said, by imperfectly credible sources, to be distantly related, although "Irish cooking" seems to be something of an oxymoron, as is "English cooking." The *Oxford* suggests *KYOO-luh-nair-ee,* as current taste suggests gluttony.

culture (KULL-chur), *n.* Something designed to transform one into something less than a complete ass. *KOOL-tchur* kisses.

cyclical (SY-kli-k'l), *adj.* Cyclic: coming around and going around. "Vicious circle" rather than "vicious cycle" is correct usage, but then there are the Hell's Angels. And if you place "en" before the first "c," you have the Pope to deal with. *SIK-lik'l* is ill, indeed.

cynic (SIH-nik), *n.* One with a solid grip on reality.

cynicism (SIH-nuh-sis'm), *n.* The flower of clinical depression. When it wilts you are considered cured, but no longer interesting.

C

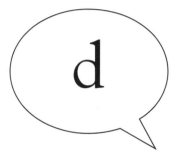

dachshund (DAHKS-hund), *n*. German for "badger dog." A small, long-bodied, short-legged dog with floppy ears. Comes standard with ground effects and good cornering capabilities.

dais (DAY-us), *n*. A raised platform for a speaker, allowing a mob unobstructed trajectory for ballistic applause. *DACE* and *DYE-iss* are the voicings of those less proficient at the hurling of cabbages at kings.

Darius (duh-RYE-us). Name of kings of ancient Persia (now ancient Iran). Darius I (the Great), 549–486 B.C.; Darius II (the Ingrate), 423–404 B.C.; and Darius III (the Not So Hot), *circa* 330 B.C. D-II also known as "the Bastard" and "the SOB" (Son of Bogoas). *DARE-ee-us* is erroneous.

data (DAY-tuh), *n*. Facts and/or figures from which specious conclusions to one's advantage can be drawn. Corps and Pols seem to prefer *DAT-uh*; Mr. Buckley is the only one who can get away with *DAH-tuh*.

deaf (DEF), *adj*. Blessed with poor hearing.

debate (dih-BAIT), *n*. In American lexicons, a word commonly draped in quotation marks or garnished with an asterisk. At Harvard, it smacks of cap and gown; in D.C., cap and bells ("presidential debate" being a favorite oxymoron of the times). *de-BAIT* and *DEE-bait* are irresolvable.

debauchery (dih-BAW-chur-ee), *n*. One of the seven signs of cultural decay, the others being rampant drug use, decline of family (Charles Manson's excepted), gluttony, digital surround sound, the fashion sense of celebrities and tourists, and the intentional shaking of Champagne bottles. A misunderstood discipline in the modern era, debauchery has fallen on hard times, especially in urban America where youth, having heeded the siren call of the gaucherie, wallow in Bud Light commercials, pointless mayhem, deep-fried Twinkies, and designer nasal sprays, while down and dirty group sex, all-night sole Veronique bashes, full-contact croquet, nude readings from the *Symposium,* and whiskey and cigars are left to wither on the vine. Well, maybe on *some* vines. *duh-BAWK-ur-ee* not.

debris (duh-BREE), *n.* Remains, leftovers, foreskins (*duh-BRIS*), etc. *DAY-bree* is okay by me.

debut (day-BYOO), *n.* 1. First public appearance of an actor, actress, stage show, play, sitcom, rock group, etc. 2. Last public appearance of an actor, actress, stage show, play, sitcom, rock group, etc. Also the arrival, with pomp (and the pompous), into polite society of a debutante who hopes that there will be a ball afterward, or before, or perhaps during. *DAY-byoo* without balls.

d

decal (dee-KAL, DEE-kal), *n*. A transferred or transferable image, picture, message, etc., for the *desecoration* of windows, vehicles, or any innocent surface. The word is short for "decalcomania," which may be instructive.

décolletage (day-kah-luh-TAZH), *n*. A neckline plunging lower than an Enron stock future. *DECK-o-luh-TAZH* hangs a little looser.

de Leon (day lee-OWN), **Ponce** (PAHN-suh) (1460–1521). Spanish explorer blamed for the discovery of West Palm Beach and the fountains of youths at Fort Lauderdale. *duh-LEE-un* works in the malls of West Palm.

deluged (DELL-youjd), *adj*. Swamped; buried; hard at it; busier than a urologist at a retirement resort. *de-LOOHJD*, by the shallows.

demagogue (DEM-uh-gawg), *n*. One willing to try new appeals to prejudice in seeking (or retaining) power, the Repubagogue being satisfied with the old.

demigod (DEH-ma-gawd), *n.* The offspring of a human being and a celebrity. *deh-ME* is belly trendy and indeed quite celebritous.

democracy (dih-MA-kru-see), *n.* A regime contingent upon full bellies and empty heads.

depot (DEEP-o), *n.* A place where a bus or train is nine hours late. In Boomerese, a *DEEP-o* is also a facility where building and home improvement supplies can be requisitioned and where WWII and Korea vets can be heard mumbling "It's *DEP-o*, asshole!" under their breath.

deputy (DEP-u-tee), *n.* A minor official whose waistline usually exceeds his authority.

derriere (dair-e-AIR), *n.* What's behind the American dieting craze.

Descartes (day-KART), **René** (1596–1650). French mathematician and philosopher. If his famous postulate, "I think, therefore I am," were applied to the twenty-first century, Noam Chomsky and I would miss the rest of you losers.

deteriorate (dih-TIER-e-uh-rate), *v.t.* To degenerate, decline, coarsen; to lose quality, status, or syllables; to achieve at one's own rate. *de-TIER-e-ate* is commonly *herd*.

Detroit (dih-TROYT), *n.* A place that regularly three-peats as the Most Dangerous City in the USA. Main industries are the manufacture of ambulances, fire engines, bandages, body armor, bulletproof glass, crutches, splints, body bags, and hypodermic needles. Current construction boom centers around funeral homes, morgues, emergency rooms, and a daycare center for the mayor. *DEE-troyt* is the southern pronunciation, that is, Canadian.

diaper (DIE-pur), *n.* From the French "diapre," meaning "ornamented cloth." Currently, a lower body wrap rather predictably ornamented. (At times, a garment suggested as an appropriate headdress for U.S. foreign-policy makers.)

Dias (DE-uhs), **Bartholomeu** (circa 1450–1500). Portuguese explorer and navigator; discoverer of "Cape of Storms" in South Africa (renamed "Cape of

Good Hope" by landlubber image consultants). *DE-az*, Anglowise.

diaspora (die-AS-puh-ruh), *n*. Originally, the scattering (dispersion) of the Jews outside of Palestine after the Babylonian exile and the destruction of the Temple (586 B.C.), resulting in the widespreading of culture, law, and one-liners, which, in turn, served to draw Eurasians down from the trees and out of the caves (well, most Eurasians). *dee-us-POOR-uh* is poor form.

dilettante (DILL-uh-tahnt), *n*. One with familiarity of everything and knowledge of nothing. Very clubbable.

Diogenes (die-AH-juh-neez) (circa 320 B.C.). Greek philosopher. Lived in a tub while searching for an honest realtor. *DI-o-JEE-nees* is too homely.

diphtheria (dif-THEER-ee-a), *n*. A particularly ugly infectious disease, hence a good one to wish upon those defrauding your pension plan, encouraging white supremacists, prescribing against your sherry intake, or disrupting your usual four hours of sleep.

diphthong (DIF-thawng), *n*. An intricate phonetic sound made by gliding from one vowel sound to another within the same syllable, as in "anoint" (to elect) or "louse" (one elected). The popular but incorrect *DIP-thong* should in no way be associated with the formal footwear of Southern Californians.

dirigible (DEAR-uh-juh-b'l), *n*. A gasbag larger than a senator. Synonym for "blimp." *adj*. Able to be steered, lobbied, or bought (cheaply). *duh-RIJ-uh-b'l* suffices.

disaster (dih-ZAS-tur), *n*. A time of grievous circumstance filled with destruction and death, in the aftermath of which egregious frauds—dwarfing the usual—are perpetrated, while looting and rape (insurance) proceed(s) apace.

disaster movie, *phr*. "Celluloid" rather true to the genre, not to mention the reviews.

Disney (DIZ-nee), *n*. According to the NYSE, a laughing stock.

divan (de-VAN), *n*. In near-Oriental domains, a

council or council room. Also *DI-van* or *dih-VAN*, a large armless, backless sofa designed for mindless, harmless "fun."

do-gooder (DOO-good-ur), *n.* One who sees your duty and does it. A body busier than the graft, corruption, and fraud that thrive on it would seem to require.

Donne (DUNN), **John** (1572–1631). Preeminent English "metaphysical" poet of his time; greatly influenced many twentieth-century versificators, not to mention alternative lexicographers. Name occasionally mispronounced as *DAHN* or *DAHN-ee*, mostly by twenty-first-century Mass Communications Ph.D. candidates and certain former Yalie flight officers from Texas whose Air National Guard records are allegedly suspect. ("Done to Donne?" is J. G. Trent's rather clever crossword clue designed to leave the unlettered up the creek without an "o'er.")

Don Quixote (kee-HO-tay). Cervantes's comic hero who, in the company of the trusty Sancho Panza, wreaked chivalry upon the land. He fell victim to a pastoral life. *KWIKS-it* is a modern fixit.

d

Dostoyevsky (DAWS-tuh-YEV-skee), **Fyodor** (FEE-uh-door) **Mikhailovich** (me-KY-luh-vitch) (1821–1881). Russian writer who described the human soul in terms of the prevailing Eurasian literary climate, that is, "cold and humorless." Both spelling *and* pronunciation—not to mention understanding (for the Yanks)—are problemthematical.

dotage (DOUGH-tij), *n.* Senility; ex *poise* facto; a condition of the aged, or those whose memory of the mendacity of kin, the inconstancy of friends, the duplicity of colleagues, the arrogance of superiors, the clatter of youth, the sanctimony of politicos, the bluster of sportsmen, the divinity of celebrities, the humility of critics, the innocence of clerics, the hypocrisy of the anointed, and the tedium of "fun" is on the wane. *DAH-tij,* nottage.

Drac Shac, *phr.* Blood bank.

drawing and quartering, *n.* An underrated and quite underused criminal rehabilitant wherein the offender's payments on his debt to society can be stretched out. An ideal correctional measure for dealing with the indiscretions of the cyber-crook, I.D. thief, professional witness, Aryan Brotherhoodlum, etc.

drawl (DRAWL), *n.* Speech free of the encumbrances of enunciation, articulation, and alacrity. As distinguished from "dialect," or a regional language variant embracing less recognizable platitudes—both patois frequently accompanied by a banjo.

dude (DOOHD), *n.* A dud scoring just above an "f."

duodenum (doo-uh-DEE-numb), *n.* The dyspeptic connection between bellyachers and internists. In the bowelry of certain British upper households, the condition is said to be commonly aggravated by a flare-up of Ulster's.

dynasty (DYE-nuh-stee), *n.* A succession of rulers from the same family, soap opera, or aristo*crassy* (incest is not frowned upon), as in the Egyptian pharaohs, the Chicago Daleys, or the Bell baseball dynasty: Buddy Bell, Albert Belle, Mike Bell, Rob Bell, Derek Bell, Jay Bell, David Bell, and etc. *DIN-uh-stee*, Britwise.

d

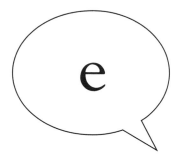

ebullient (ih-BOOL-yuhnt), *adj.* Insufferably enthusiastic, effervescent, bubbly, bubble-headed. From the Latin "ebulliere," meaning "to boil." Unfortunately, the exact substance in which the Romans preferred to boil the bubbly has been lost to antiquity.

éclair (ay-KLAIR), *n.* French for "lightning." Hence, an electric discharge of atmospheric custard from a cloud of egg pastry streaked with chocolate. According to the surgeon general, consumption of more than four at a sitting is considered a bit hoggy. *EE-klair* for those who can stop at three.

economical (eh-kuh-NAH-mih-kul), *adj.* Crummy enough to fall under the heading of ersatz (*AIR-sahts*), to qualify as a tract home, or to appeal to those who have to ask the price of a four-dollar California claret selling for twenty-five. *ECH!-uh-NAH-muh-kul* works for the latter.

economics (eh-kuh-NAH-miks), *n.* A pursuit fraught with economists. *ek-uh-NAH-miks* is often heard as the science tends more toward art, as well as "Hey, I'm not making this up, folks, there is actually a Nobel Prize offered in this category!" Synonym is "Meteorology."

Edinburgh (Eh-d'n-bur-uh), *n.* Capital of Caledonia, near the Firth of Forth and a fifth of Scotch. Center of learning, culture, biscuits. Robert Burns once slept there; Samuel Johnson regularly fell asleep there. *ED'n-burg* is acceptable, if you roll your rrrs.

education (eh-juh-KAY-shun), *n*. The ongoing and lifelong process by which the volume of mush in one's head is reduced by one-third. *eh-jih-KAY-shun* and *ED-yooh-KAY-shun* pass, too.

eggplant (EHG-plant), *n*. Chicken coop. Also the vegetable responsible for the invention of heavy sauces.

8-Mile Road, *phr*. Eminem Domain.

either / neither (EEH-thur, NEE-thur or EYE-thur, NYE-thur), *adjs., conjs., advs., etc*. Either is correct; neither is incorrect; both being suitable at times.

electronics (ih-lek-TRAH-niks), *n*. The prosthesis giving voice and instrumentality to modern popular-ists, metallicals, etc. It is said to generally aid modern man in his quest for self-ful*frill*ment. *e-lek-TRAH-niks* is acceptable, sort of.

eleven (ih-LEH-vun), *n*. In Warsaw, Chicago, or Hamtramck, a baker's dozen. Also, the number of Americans who know the name of the prime minister of Canada and/or the president of Mexico, or the number of middle school students who know *where* Mexico is. (Note: At least twice as many Canadian middle school students know the name of the Canadian P.M.) Most citizens will pronounce this as *LEV-in* or *e-LEH-vin*, both of which are kosher by me.

elite (ay-LEET, ih-LEET, ee-LEET), *n.* The elect; the best. The bestials of history include the Nazi SS, the Inquisitors, and Saddam Hussein's Elite Republican Guard (now said to be on hiatus). In America, the elite are determined by their access to liver transplants over people with more legitimate needs, and are easily recognizable in restaurants as those engaged in Chateau Lafaurie-Peyraguey chugalugging contests, with the side-orders of truffles next to the cheeseburgers.

embedded with, *phr.* "Attached to" for those who schlep with the enemy, i.e., network ninnies, media madmen, and language louts.

Empedocles (em-PEH-duh-kleez). Fifth century B.C. Greek philosopher who held that everything, with the possible exception of Utah, is composed of the "prime" elements: earth, air, and firewater. *em-PEH-duh-k'lz* is popular among the massage therapist caste, binge smilers, realtors-in-training, Carolinians, and forward units of the Boomer generation.

emu (EE-myoo), *n.* A large Australian bird with useless wings, similar to the Iraqi, Irani, and Syrian air forces. All approaching extinction. *EE-mooh* is pooh.

enclave (EN-klave), *n.* 1. An enclosed unit or compound; 2. Foreign territory surrounded by a particular country (Washington, D.C., for example). *AHN-klave* is not so particular.

enlibra (en-LEE-bruh), *n.* Republican for "in balance," especially in regard to the environment. A word conned by factional anesthetists while attempting to put the body politic even farther under than usual. Efforts at revivifaction and habilitonement were unsuckupful. *ahn-LEE-bruh*, by the perpe*traitors*.

ennui (ahn-WEE), *n.* Boredom. In the USA, discretionary time filled by felonious driving, recreational litigation, body-piercing, chat rooms, channel-surfing for exciting soccer, questioning the divinity of network news anchors, and the search for an honest crab cake—attended by pharmaceutical adventurism, pandering, blood sports, the trafficking in aftermarket appendages, and general noise-making. *AHN-way* and the captivating *EN-u-I* being part of the latter.

en route (ahn ROOT), *phr.* Lucky to have gotten away, i.e. from Atlanta, Gary, St. Louis, Baltimore, Detroit, Thousand Oaks, Compton, Amherst, Newton, Birmingham, Liverpool, or Sunnyvale.

entrepreneur (ahn-truh-pruh-NUHR), *n.* A player; a low-grade producer of secreted hazardous waste and/or street drugs but still able to buy off the Feds. A magnate for organized labor, as in Conan Doyle's "He was a typical London tradesman: obese, pompous, and slow." In Grosse Pointe or Newport Beach, a teen who sells it but doesn't use it.

envelope (EN-vuh-lope), *n.* A smallish cover-up. In the Progressive era, a wrapper containing good news, for instance, that spinster aunt Elvira died but did not leave it all to the kitties as she had previously threatened to do in the presence of the covetous vultures passing for family, who could now "get that Harley," "get that nose job," "get that purer coke," get, get, get, etc. Envelopes attain to glory by being "pushed." The human envelope is called "skin," a mostly thin substance that, according to the CDC (Committee for Doughnuts and Circuses), has been pushed to the limit in certain venues of the industrialized hemisphere. *AHN-vuh-lope* is second best but first used.

envoy (EN-voy), *n.* A messenger-boy delegated to represent one government in its misdealings with another, while almost always being immune to diplomacy. An envoy generally ranks above an attaché but level with the behind of an ambassador. *AHN-voy* is trendy but a bit off.

épée (EH-pay), *n.* A long, tapered blood-sport instrument, shorter than a hockey stick wielded by a little league dad with a prominent vocabulary of profanities, upon whom *uh-PEE* should be taken.

epoch (EH-puhk), *n*. A time in the progression of man and the ascendancy of reason commencing with an important date (historically ornamented by a bomb) and ending with an equally important date (historically ornamented by a bigger bomb). *EE-pahk, ee-PAHK*, no.

equestrienne (ih-kwess-tree-ENN), *n*. A woman who performs with a horse, which is quite a sight. Catherine the Great and Lady Godiva come to mind. *ee-KWESS-tree-in*, neighhhh.

equinox (EE-kwuh-nahks), *n*. A time of year when day and night are equally tedious and when astrologers and certain members of the Screen Actors Guild are able to stand an egg on end. (The bacon is slightly more difficult.) Echh! for *EK-win-ahks*.

eras (EER-uhz), *n*. Periods of history liberally sprinkled with "begots," "ushered-ins," "markeds," and "engendereds." For instance: "Men's T-shirt/suit coat fashion combo *begot* the era of the slob" (or vice versa); "1980s factionalism *ushered in* an era of political atavism"; "The invention of the video game *marked* the era of mindlessness"; or "*Playboy* magazine *engendered* the era of penicillin." *AIR-uhz* and *EE-ruhz* are faulty.

err (EHR), *v.* To mistake, or to forget to cover up a mistake. *AIR* and *URR* also work.

erudite (ERR-uh-dite, ERR-yuh-dite), *adj.* Wretchedly learned; unsettlingly knowledgeable. A word in the American public-education lexicon seeking, since 1965, both pronunciation and direction. *ERR-ooh-dite* and the rather fragrant *AIR-e-u-dite* are clinkerish (at this time).

esoteric (eh-suh-TAIR-ik), *adj.* Understood only by a chosen few or other esoterrorists, cultists, matrix d's, rap-scallions, tax authors, symbolic logicians, officers of the court, Sponge Bobophiles, and those who play James Dean movies backward, receive subliminal messages from collectible Burma Shave signs, are in regular contact with the moons of Neptune, or extrapolate yesterday's headlines from the "Bible code." "Hit for the cycle," "player interference," "balk," "triple witching," "triple-double," "magic number," and "the spread" are just some of the esotericisms used by smug sports reporters when encrypting the highlights. *eh-so-TAIR-ik,* no.

ethics (EH-thiks), *n.* A code of conduct recommended by politicians, attorneys, and churchmen to their opponents.

Ettinger (ET-eeng-ur, ET-in-jur), **R. C. W.** Author of the seminal work *The Prospect of Immortality* and one of the founders of cryonics, or the preservation of wealthy corpses until the coming of the Power Failure.

Eurydice (yoo-RID-uh-see). The wife of Orpheus. After she was killed and delivered to the underworld, Orpheus gained permission to bring her back from Hades (*HAY-deez*) via Orlando, but she was forced to return because Orpheus broke his agreement with Pluto by hiring a private detective to see if she was followed by Mickey or Goofy.

euthanasia (YOO-thuh-NAY-zhuh), *n.* A more promising treatment employed when surgery fails.

evil (EE-vul), *n.* The evening clothes of foolishness. *EE-vill!!* and *EE-vile!!* are the property of mail-order pastors, righteous tract passers, and other sandwich-board saints.

evolution (eh-vuh-LOO-shun), *n.* The progression and advancement of species, such as worms to toads, toads to shrews, shrews to apes, apes to men, and men to jack-asses. *EE-vuh-LOO-shun* is more British than correct.

exorcism (EK-sawr-sih-z'm), *n.* The drawing-off of excess evil from the soulless and possessed, that is, non-tithing Baptists, Mormons, and other "polluted" parishioners. It is performed by raising the voice and scaring the hell out of the Devil.

expatriate (ek-SPAY-tree-ate), *v.* To neuter the polit-ically cocky by unceremoniously shipping them from, say, Panama or Cuba or Baghdad to an accepting third-world venue such as Miami or Los Angeles, where they will no longer pose a threat to the estab-lished corruption. *n. ek-SPAY-tree-it:* a connected Yankee in Queen Arthur's Bermuda.

expertise (ek-spur-TEEZ), *n*. The pathology of the anointed. Experts and specialists are quite synonymous in that they are generally those who leave the smallest number of surgical instruments in the chest cavity, or those able to precisely assess the number and kind of weapons of mass destruction in Iraq. A case in point is the infamous orthopod Dr. Procopious, who was such an expert in his specialty that even his E-mail was illegible. *eks-pur-TEECE* is faulty.

extraordinary (ik-STRAWR-d'n-er-ee), *adj*. Special; exceptional; especially distinguished. The Law of Diminishing Modifiers now allows the word to be used even in reference to professional athletes, both "recovering" and "clean," in which case the extra-special pronunciation of *ik-struh-OR-d'n-er-ee* applies.

exuberance (ig-ZOO-bur-uns), *n*. A common defect of character in those prone to exhibitions of "salesmanship," fits of social awareness, or other excesses, dissipations, theme parties, and fund-raisers. According to Professor Backwootuh, of Queensland, the problem is correctable by exiling brunch hostesses and motivational speakers for a period of seven years.

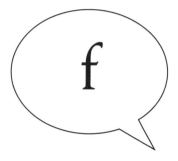

facade (fuh-SAHD), *n*. A front; or, in the spirit of the times, a false front built up from ornamental steel, limestone, silicone, deceptive accountants, edificial egomaniacs, etc., as is the case with certain free-wheeling republics hosted by the Statue of Libertine and in which ads for bosom-boosters and penis-stiffeners are the most common offerings of the Internet. (Quick, where's my mouse?!) *fuh-KAID* and

FUCK-aid are the pronouncements of techno tubbies, options orphans, and the usual superficial sillies.

fait accompli (FAY-tuh-kom-PLEE). French for "accomplished fact." Hence, "that's that"; "over and done with"; "no need to pound it further into the ground on the 11 o'clock news," etc. This expression was struck from political lexicons in the nineteenth century.

fakir (fuh-KEER), *n*. A Muslim beggar and holy man who claims to perform miracles. The closest Western equivalent seems to be "Televangelist-with-a-Bad-Do-and-Funny-Clothes," although "Day-Trading Guru," "Magnetic Therapist," "Homeland Security Director," "Shamway Recruiter Who Can Show You the Shining Path to Financial Independence in Five Years or Less," and "Candidate With Sure-Fire Plan to Reduce the Deficit and Rescue Social Security and Medicare" are not far behind. *FAKE-ur* and *FUH-kir*, for some reason, seem to be the preferred popular variations worldwide.

falcon (FAL-k'n, FAWL-k'n), *n*. Any hawk or hawklike bird, with curved, notched beak and claws. In other words, a predator resembling your eighth-grade math teacher. Sportscasters say *FELL-k'n*, which doesn't add up. (Sorry, Atlanta! And, oh yes, same to you, Mrs. O'Hara!)

fame, *n*. The relentless pursuit of media-ocrity.

fatuous (FA-choo-us), *adj*. Said of those who "chew the fat" until it bleeds. Popular fat-laden expressions of lardheads are: "level the playing field," "my promise to you," "defendant showed no emotion," "fell through the cracks," "due to," "the American people," "the American dream," "now, maybe we can have closure," "the healing process can begin," "a free gift," "can't we all just get along!," etc.

Favre (FARV), **Brett** (1969–). Noted professional football quarterback with surname made to order for dyslexic sportscasters. *FARV* is gotten from "Favre" in the same way that *luh-FEE-vur* is distilled from "Lefebvre" and *FEB-you-air-e* is wrenched from "February."

FBI, *n*. A rather suspicious anagram.

February (FEH-byuh-wair-ee, FEH-bruh-wair-ee), *n.* The month of the year requiring the squeezing of 31 days of folly into 28, quadrennially excepted. *FEB-you-air-ee*, a phonemic dissimilation (huh?), is popularly acceptable. The original verse is:

> *Thirty days hath November,*
> *April, June, and September,*
> *February hath twenty-eight alone,*
> *And all the rest have thirty-wone.*

feces (FEE-seez), *n. pl.* Solid excreta. Unless, of course, one is regularly caught up in the allure of the taco stand, the salad bar, the mobile lunch wagon, or Denny's. There is no singular feces; however, certain theocrats, teen "idols," telemarketers, I.D. thieves, and Hollywood agents are rank enough for nomination. . . .

fecund (FEH-kund), *adj.* A more carnal cognate of "prolific." Humans were not particularly prolific until they started seriously fecunding-around during the beginning of the fifteenth century, when the French introduced an alternative type of body odor and the barbarians founded cheap Cologne. *FEE-kund*, now and then.

feminists, *n.* Weapons of "Miss" destruction.

fender, *n.* A cloakwheelism.

fiat (FEE-ut), *n.* A dictatorial pronouncement by legally constituted authority in the absence of representative government, such as at the dinner table, in the mini-van, oval office, boardroom, courtroom, platoon, etc. *FEE-aht* is passable.

fidelity (fuh-DEL-uh-tee), *n.* Accuracy or faithfulness, as in "The congressman plagiarized Oliver Wendell Holmes with absolute fidelity" or "He played the cuckold with complete fidelity." *fy-DEL-uh-ete* is screwy.

fifty cents (FIFF-tee SENTS), *n.* The price of a nickel phone call or a 10-cent newspaper; a down payment on a two-bit greeting card. *FITTY-SENT* is not *fit* for comment.

finis (FIH-nus, FIE-nus), *n.* The word preceding the credits of "art" films, or those motion pictures wherein the "end" is quite apparent before the finish. *FIN-is* is the usual misvoicing.

flatulence (FLAH-chuh-lunts), *n*. A prostate toot, in men; in women with a certain air about them, the toot is typically sublimated (dangerously silent), causing a swelling of the Xanthippial cortex, which can be relieved by washing the hair, dumping a boyfriend, or viewing a recent rerun of Dr. Phil. According to credibility activist Geraldo Rivera, starlets, interns, royals, and celebrities recently profiled on *Inside the Actors' Studio* are immune to this condition.

fog (FAWG), *n*. A layer of air that hovers from about 5'3" to 7'1" off the ground, in most civilized societies. According to Professor Nimbus, it is composed of elements of phenepherines, caffeines, salicylates, phenols, barbiturates, cocas, colas, cannabises, acetaminophens, mouthwash, bayrum, and microchips. *FAHG* was Harold's favorite.

folic (FOE-lik), *adj*. Of folic acid, used to treat non-literary anemia. Good sources of folic acid are said to be freshly squeezed orange juice, freshly squeezed clam juice, and vitamin B. *FAHL-ik* is folly.

forbade (fur-BAD), *v.t.* The past tense of "forbid," a stimulus to action.

forte (FORT), *n.* One's strong point; what one does particularly well, despite one's pathetic education, broken family, popular addictions, laziness, and exposure to daytime TV. The celebrity's forte, for example, is his/her faculty for mispronouncing the word as *for-TAY* or *FOR-tay* (meaning "loud").

Frankenstein (FRANG-kun-stine, -steen, -shtine, -shteen, etc.), *n.* Monster's ink, i.e., a novel by Mary W. Shelley.

Freud (FROYD), **Sigmund** (1856–1939). Austrian neurologist/psychologist. "Father of psychoanalysis." Concluded that men want honor, power, and the love of women. Died perplexed as to what women want. *FROOD* is rude, dood.

fungi (FUN-ji), *n.* Plural of "fungus" (FUNG-gus). Rootless, leafless, flowerless, colorless plant life, including toadstools, mildews, molds, multi-level marketers, etc. (Paramecia, terrorists, telemarketers, anti-Semitists, Klansmen, child molesters, and ex-governors of the state of Arizona fall under the heading of protozoa.) *FUN-guy* and *FUN-gus-iz* are good for a laugh but only marginally acceptable.

fuselage (FYOO-suh-lawzh), *n.* The part of a wide-bodied or jumbo aircraft containing wide-bodied or jumbo American passengers, the parts of which have been *fused* together. Currently, *FEW-suh-lahzh*.

fusillade (FYOO-suh-lade), *n.* Rapid and continuous discharge, not unlike a Chris Matthews interview or what occurred after they broke into the Viagra cabinet at the nursing home.

gala (GAY-luh), *n*. Noise-making with the excuse of charity, over which hangs the cloud of enthusiasm. As at the Oscars, tasteful dress is optional. *GAH-luh* and *GAL-uh* are equally optional.

Galileo (gah-luh-LEE-o) **Galilei** (1564–1642). Italian astronomer and physicist; invented telescope; condemned for heresy by the Inquisition for not inventing binoculars. *Gal-uh-LAY-o* is popular among laymen.

garage (guh-RAHZH), *n.* A housing that keeps your ride safe and clean for the carjacker. Ever hear the one about the part-time Brooklyn grease monkey? He always went home oily. *guh-RAHJ* and the British *GAIR-ij* are both honest alternatives.

garage sale, *phr.* For some reason, even professional sign-makers invariably omit the "B" from this placard (*PLAH-kurd*).

garrote (guh-RAHT), *n.* A Spanish collar designed by rather single-minded eighteenth-century couturiers and used in dressing-down adversaries to the state's fashion. *v.t.* To employ a cord, wire, or other ligature in properly addressing the indifference of a bureaucrat or inducing more precise accounting in the shopper in front of you who's trying to pass a third-party check for 23 items in the 8 Items or Less lane. *GAR-et* and *guh-ROTE* are breathtakingly wrong.

gauche (GOESH), *adj.* Of a level of social sophistication aspired to by entry-level slovens and other goateens, gang-bangers, gay bashers, hipsters, ravers, happenin'ees, boom-boxers, box Boomers, tourists, soccer fans, sloganeers, and inveterate smilers. *GOWSH*—ouch!

gauntlet (GAWNT-let), *n.* Middle English for "gantelet" ("glove"). An armored glove. The obsolete "gantlet," a corruption of "gantlope," which is a corruption of "gatlopp," referred to a type of military punishment—distinct from being forced to dine in a mess hall—wherein an offender was required to run between two lines of men strategically equipped to impede his progress and who, afterward, may indeed have appeared to be a bit *gaunt*. Gauntlet thus serves correctly as both glove and run.

g

genomics (jee-NAH-miks), *n.* The science of whether or not to clone Alan Greenspan for the good of Western civilization. It also investigates the chromosome responsible for rendering male humans broccoli-intolerant and unable to fold fitted sheets. *jen-AH-miks* and *jen-OH-miks*, stock-optionally.

gerrymander (GAIR-ee-man-dur), *v.t.* To vigorously allow a voting district to avail itself of a more equal political footing before a Republican crook gets the same idea. After nineteenth-century Massachusetts governor Elbridge Gerry, plus 3/5 of the word "salamander" in which shape the "adjusted" precinct took form. *JAIR-ee-man-dur* is the common slander.

Gettysburg (GET-iz-burg), *n.* Pennsylvania town known for a two-hour, fifty-seven-and-a-half-minute speech delivered by ex-senator Edward Everett on November 19, 1863. (A tall, gaunt Kentuckian addressed the crowd for the remainder of the three-hour gig.) *GET-eez-burg*, optionally.

ghoti (FISH), *n.* George Bernard Shaw's conundrumous ichthyogram calling attention to the inconsistencies in English spelling and pronunciation, he having been a foremost proponent of phonetic orthography. It combines the "gh" of "enough" with the "o" of "women" and the "ti" of "action" = go "fish!"

Giamatti (jah-MAH-tee), **A. Bartlett** (1938–89). Former commissioner of major league baseball; his censuring of Cincinnati Reds player Pete Rose for alleged gambling violations is said to have caused him immense emotional hardship. *jee-uh-MAH-tee* is conventional but not Italian enough.

gigolo (JIH-guh-low), *n*. A fee male.

gimcrack (JIM-krak), *n*. That separating the American consumer from a worthy bank account and a reputation for good taste. Repositories for older gimcracks are called antique shops, estate sales, Smithsonians, dumpsters, etc. Synonyms are QVC-krak and EBAY-krak. *GIM-krak* is correctless.

Gloucester (GLOSS-tur), *n*. Earl of. A Shakespearean character who sets up a shelter for homeless kings suffering from Gonerilla. All other ills as usual are blamed on King Lear's other daughter. Also, an English city on the Severn.

gnocchi (NYAWK-ee), *n*. An Italian dumpling distinct from Francesca Gregorini or Giada de Laurentiis. Gina Lollobrigida, for you older droolers. From the Greek "gnothi," meaning to know a tomato from a dumpling. *NOOK-ee* is the two-star version.

gnu (NOO, NYOO), *n.* A large African antelope resembling a horse but with a thick neck and an oxlike head (shorter at the shoulder than a linebacker, a Farrakhan bodyguard, or a Teamsters' business agent). *guh-NOO*, g'not.

golf (GAWLF), *n.* A recreational activity in which men are said to "attack their balls." Aside from the curious eraserless pencil, equipment includes a "mashie," a "brassie," a "niblick," and a nudnick. The exact origin of the discipline is uncertain; however, over the years, cryptically odd terms have attached themselves to the ritual, such as "metal wood," "lie," "trap," "press," "putz," "hazard," "gimmie," "par ousia," "foursome," and "gruesome," which the author has taken the trouble to trace to radical elements of the Balata tree worshippers of West India and Southern New Guinea. Following a "round" of golf, men sit in a "clubhouse" revising their "scorecards" while preparing for a "DWI," having left their equipment at the "bag drop" to be cleaned and "filched" by "caddies." *GAWF, GAHLF* (Arnie's favorite), and the Back Bay beauty *GAFF* are also acceptable at most "handicapped" institutions.

golf car(t), *n.* Misusage rather than mispronunciation is the issue here. There *is* such a thing as a golf *cart* and there *is* such a thing as a golf *car*. The difference is power. A golf *car* is self-powered, using either an electric motor or a gasoline engine, and carries golf clubs and one or more "duffers." A golf *cart* carries golf clubs only and is *carted* (pulled or pushed) by a golfer. Alas, these days anything that prowls a golf course on wheels, such as the golf car containing your boss (to whom you are sucking up by allowing him to save par), is referred to as a golf "cart."

gondola (GAHN-duh-luh), *n.* A receptacle of tourism in which one is taken for a ride, either in the presence of atonality or of hot air. When hot-air ballooning, incidentally, it is always wise to include a politician or two in the party, just in case of a flame-out. *gahn-DOE-luh* is a downer.

Gorbachev (gawr-buh-CHAWF), **Mikhail Sergeyevich** (1931–). Former Soviet Premier noted for Glasnost (the first Soviet "openness"), Perestroika (the first Soviet "reform"), and Raisa (the first Soviet first lady capable of squeezing into less than a size 12 shoe). GOR-*buh-chawf*, media-wise (is that an oxymoron?).

gorilla / guerrilla (guh-RIL-uh), *n.* Fierce combatants wherein chest beating is not *Contra*-indicated for both. Both are also known to pose nicely for *National Geographic* cameras. Physical characteristics include long matted hair, repulsive body odor, crazed eyes, foul breath, and a tendency to travel about on all fours while whooping and grunting aggressively toward a prospective mate. From this, however, the *gorilla* differs quite a bit. *Webster's* gives the same pronunciation for both, while the *Oxford* is rather "o"ish on the former.

gourmand (GOOR-mahnd, -mund), *n.* A glutton. As distinguished from a "gourmet" (GOOR-*may*), who lacks capacity. It is, in any case, said to be a mutual-admiration *satiety*. *gor-MAHND* and *gor-MAY* do not go hungry in the USA.

gracile (GRASS'l), *adj.* Handsomely thin; willowy, hominidinally speaking. As distinguished from North Americans. Asians were gracile until Occidentally cross-bred with migratory Drivethruvians during the Big Boom period. *GRAY-si-ul* and *GRAY-s'l* are also in the competition for this busy, busy word.

Granada (gruh-NAH-duh), *n.* Picturesque Andalusian city in Spain, characterized by Moorish turrets and boorish tourists. Home of the monumental Alhambra, a citadel of two million square feet that approaches the Mall of America in grandeur but is easier to find your way around in. *gruh-NAY-duh* is strictly for the gringos.

grease (GREECE), *n.* The ingredient lending flavor to edibles. It is not present in the twigs, berries, and gag-goo popularly known as "health food." The reader, incidentally, should always be wary of anyone who is comfortable with *GREEZ* or *GREE-zee*. Before you know it, the fool will have you waltzing with a mop in the mess hall.

Grenada (gruh-NAY-duh), *n.* West Indies island; capital, St. George's. A 1983 invasion by airborne units of the U.S. Army, outnumbered three to one by elite elements of the U.S. press corps, ended in the surrender of six pushcart peddlers, eleven medical students, a seventy-eight-year-old hooker, and three English-speaking travel agents from Baton Rouge. *grih-NAD-uh* and *gruh-NAHD-uh* are overkill.

Gresham (GRESH-um), **Sir Thomas** (1519–79). Of Gresham's Law, stating that hard money (gold, silver, etc.) will be driven out of circulation by paper currency wherever it is found. As distinguished from "Grisham" (*GRISH-um*) and other bestselling authors of predictable, hardcover screenplays. *GRES-um* and *GRES-ham* cannot be banked.

Gretzky (GRETZ-key), **Wayne** (1961–). Lord of the rinks.

grimace (GRIH-muss), *n.* A distortion of the countenance expressive of amused pain. A common visage among judges who preside over felony celebrity cases; among film directors in the presence of a dramatic reading by a "starlet"; among reporters covering a George W. Bush speech; or among those whose casual reading list includes the Tax Code.

groceries (GROW-sur-eez), *n*. Items in a grocery (store), including such traditional staples as rice, beans, chicken wings, ladyfingers, pigs' knuckles, and butchers' thumbs. How *GROWSH* got into "grocery" or "groceries" is anybody's *guesh*.

Grosvenor (GROVE-nur). Name of a London square and gallery, the latter founded in 1877 by Sir Coutts Lindsay for the exhibition of works by accomplished ("as well as modern") artists. Also the name of American editor Gilbert H. Grosvenor (1875–1966), who put *National Geographic* magazine on the map and the map *in National Geographic* magazine. *GROSE-ven-ur*, by the square.

Guadeloupe (GWAH-d'l-oop). French-controlled islands of the Leeward group in the West Indies. Site of the Travel Agents Hall of Fame and Burial Ground. *Gwad-uh-LOOP-a*, Hispanicwise.

guidon (GUY-d'n), *n*. A military unit pennant, originally carried by the guide of a troop of U.S. mounted cavalry prior to the invention of the triptych. Custer is said to have not relied on it. *GUY-dahn* is all right, if you don't want to stop and ask for directions.

guillotine (GIL-uh-teen), *n.* A device for removing the burden of response-ability from the shoulders of the accused, the invention of which is traditionally (but erroneously) attributed to Dr. Joseph Guillotin during the French Revolution and employed in capital cases involving murder, sedition, overcooking the asparagus, etc. Similar rehabilitative instruments had been in use elsewhere several centuries earlier. *GEE-uh-teen* heads the list of popular misvoicings.

gun shop, *n.* A gat station.

gunwale (GUH-n'l), *n.* The upper side of a ship, from the quarter-deck to the forecastle, supportive of guns (cannon). Very seldom, if ever, pronounced as spelled.

guru (GUR-ooh), *n.* A personal assistant whose expertise lies in assisting himself to the bank accounts of the naïve. In America, it is heavy on the GOO. In the Orient, an instructor of the out-of-body experience; in the Occident, the out-of-mind.

gyno- (guy-nuh), *cf.* Greek for "women," from which is gotten *GAHN-uh-KAHL-uh-jest*, or one who looks into areas of women's genitourinary and rectal diseases and who may be likely to *stirrup* controversy over privacy issues.

gyro (YEE-ro), *n.* Greek for "turn" or "rotate." A New Hellenic taco consisting of thin slices of spitted (turned) lamb-beef combo in a pita pocket, garnished with a piquant cucumber-onion sauce. If plural ("gyros"), pass the Mylanta or go for the cheesecake.

g

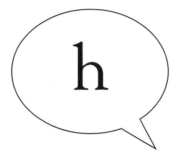

habanero (hah-bun-YAIR-o), *n.* A chile pepper served with precautionary garnishes of defibrillator and nitroglycerine tabs. Also, a Spanish slow dance (or fast, depending on how many peppers you ate). *hab-uh-NAIR-o* ain't cool.

habeas corpus (HAY-bee-us KOR-pus) *n.* Latin, meaning simply "Where's the body?" In Medellin, Baghdad, Newark, etc., "Where isn't the body?"

habitué (huh-BITCH-oo-way), *n*. A frequenter, especially of a club, bar, saloon, etc. Carla might thus ask: "So then whadda we call your kid, Lilith, a son of a habitue?" *huh-BITCH-oo-ee*, excusedly.

haggis (HAG-uss), *n*. Traditional Scottish entree consisting of the minced entrails of a sheep or calf mixed with onions, suet, and oatmeal, then boiled in the stomach of the critter. Seconds, anyone? Firsts? *HAG-eez* does not settle well, either.

halitosis (ha-luh-TOE-sus), *n*. The exhaust of small talk.

Halley (HAL-ee), **Edmund** (1656–1742). English astronomer who discovered, among other things, the proper motions of the stars two hundred years before Hedda Hopper discovered the improper. *HAIL-ee* is pop but not.

Halloween (hal-uh-WEEN), *n*. Evening of October 31, followed by "Allhallows" and the annual extinguishing of Detroit. A cautionary holiday, according to National Safety Council president Hammond

Wrigh, who claims to have once discovered an apple in his razor blades. *HAHL-uh-WEEN* is a fright.

Handel (HAN-d'l), **George** (zhorzh) **Frideric** (1685–1759). Influential English-speaking German composer of Italian operas and other multicultural musical miscellanea. Died Baroque. *HAHN-d'l* is incorrect because it does not reflect the German umlaut "a" in the original spelling of his name. So there!

hara-kiri (har-ih-KIHR-ee), *n.* Traditional Japanese ceremony to which the adage "practice makes perfect" does not apply (except in certain Slavic venues). It is a rather final ritual used by the elite to avoid disgrace, execution, or, worse, a Senate confirmation hearing. *HAIR-ee-KAIR-ee* is incorrect, except around Wrigley Field, of course.

harass (HAIR-us), *v.* To systematically bother (an adversary), as does a drill sergeant who trained under an IRS agent, who trained under a paparazzo, who trained under your wife. *her-ASS*, nevertheless, is quite popular.

h

Hawai'i (huh-WAH-ye), *n.* A large concentration of airliners and cruise ships in the North Pacific, surrounded by pineapple (at this writing). Climate is temperate (there reportedly hasn't been a nip in the air since the winter of 1941). Second favorite expression of natives is "aloha," meaning "hello." Favorite expression of natives is "aloha," meaning "goodbye." State flower: hibiscus. State fish: humuhumunukunukuapawaha. State bird: Boeing 747. *huh-WI-e* is common, *huh-WI-yuh* is acceptable only from southern hoosiers, *HI-WI-uh* through the Iowa, Missouri, Arkansas corridor.

Haydn (HYE-d'n), **Franz Joseph** (1732–1809). Austrian composer; close friend of Mozart; prolific composer of symphonae and sonatae. The Haydn Sikh Society of Vienna and East Punjab regularly commemorates his birth, celebrating the composer's oratorios with a community Singh. *HAY-d'n* is incorrect, except among hayseeds.

helicopter (HELL-uh-kahp-tur), *n.* "Rotary wing" flying machine. Used extensively during the Vietnam War (1964–). Modern U.S. "attack" helicopters are equipped with "night vision" technology, which, according to Field Grade Rotarian General Tommy "Hotdog" Franx, enables the pilot to better see which other "attack" helicopter it is colliding with, which defective spare part causes it to crash, or which "RPG" insurgent it is being shot down by. *HE-luh-kahp-tur* and *HE-lee-uh-kahp-tur* are inauspicious. *CHAH-pur* is more like it. *HE-LOW* in naval lingo.

hemorrhoid (HEM-royd, HEM-uh-royd), *n*. Also known as "Osamarrhoid." A grave affliction butt for hydrocortisone acetate, suppositorially.

herb (URB), *n*. Any of many superfluous vegetables that tend to pollute the sufficient salt and pepper of meat and potatoes. According to ex-Canadian proper-person-in-chief Prof. Peter Jenningz, this pronunciation is just another step toward the total yokelization of the English language by the basically bumpkinish lower 48ers, not to mention an insult to his favorite ancient soft rockers Peaches & Herb. North-of-the-border provincials sound the "h"— HURB—as do the Baker Street regulars, where, in the melodrama *Terror By Night*, for instance, the bumbleton inspector Lestrade, as interlocutor, asks Watson " 'Oo, 'im?" "Yes. *'im*, that's *'oo!*"

herbalist (UR-buh-list), *n.* A grass-roots activist. An expert in herbs, especially an herbalist who experiments with or cultivates medicinal herbs, succeeding usually by *trowel* and error.

herbicide (UR-buh-side), *n.* Any agent used to destroy or slow down the growth of objectional weeds, radishes, okra, goatees, etc.

heretic (HAIR-uh-tik), *n.* One having removed his gas mask in the presence of the foul air of orthodoxy. Formerly, a religious dissenter easily burned-up over dogma. *huh-RET-ik* is the discorrectest.

hermaphrodite (hur-MAF-ruh-dyte), *n.* Equal-opportunity orgasmism; double-duty booty. *hur-MORF-uh-dyt* is unfortunately all too common.

hermitage (HUR-muh-tij), *n.* Where resides a hermit. *hur-muh-TAHZH* is reserved for a residence containing a Rubens, a wet bar, and a hermitess (or three). Hef would approve.

hernia (HUR-nee-uh), *n*. In females, the protrusion of part of a bowel through the stomach wall. It is erroneously thought to occur as a result of lifting overweight or ponderous objects, such as anvils, juristic egos, federal budget proposals, or Texans. In males, "hisnia" (*HIZ-nee-uh*).

hero (HERE-o), *n*. One having performed a courageous and selfless act, despite one's preference for the greedy, gluttonous, profane, lustful, loud, arrogant, pandering, hectoring, sports-besotted lifestyle. A temporary expatriate of diffidence. *HE-roe*, in Thessalonica and Jockswap, West Virginia.

Himalayas (hih-muh-LAY-uhs), *n*. A mountain range lying between Tibet and India and containing Mt. Everest, the highest (29,028 feet) junkyard in the world (near-space excepted). Everest was first successfully littered in 1953 by Sir Edmund Hillary and Tenzing Norgay, the sherpa of things to come. *hih-MAHL-yuhz* is also correct, sort of.

Hired hand, *n*. A farm assist.

h

Hiroshima (hir-uh-SHE-muh). Major city on Honshu, Japan's largest island, pronunciation of which often borders on blastphemy. *hir-uh-SHE-muh, hih-RO-shuh-muh, HERE-o-SHE-muh* . . . you'll hear them all.

hirsute (HUR-soot), *adj.* Hairy; bristly; shaggy, beardy, weirdy. Chiefly describing young men of more fame than fortune who evidently have suffered a falling-out with the gods of grooming. ("Cosmo" and the other Sacred Texts insist that little girls swoon over them.) *HEER-soot,* optionally.

homage (AH-mij), *n.* Worshipful reverence, veneration, or enormous respect paid a) to a lord by a vassal; b) to a tabloid by an American; c) to a TV camera by an Al Sharpton. (Homage was once paid to Mr. Dukakis and Mr. Gingrich but it is now said to be in the hands of a collection agency.) *HAH-mij* is not even funny.

homicide (HAH-muh-side), *n.* The killing of one or more human beings by one or more other human beings, for fun and/or profit. In Michigan and D.C., a second and more serious charge is filed if a firearm—rather than a bayonet, ice pick, garrote, pit bull, Mercedes, fire bomb, Burmese python, nude photo of Norman Mailer, etc.—is used. Spousal homicide against females is legal in South America and the Middle East, if you bring a note from your clergyman, and in Rockingham Drive, with a note from your publicist. (For more information, please contact www.ojay/ex&beau.org.y.) *HOE-muh-side* is just murder.

hoof (HOOF, HUHF), *n. pl.* The foot or feet of horses, cattle, deer, etc. Preceded by "cloven" when referring to members of the Executive, Legislative, or Judicial animal farms.

hospital (HAHS-pih-t'l), *n.* A house of ills' repute.

hostage (HAHS-tij), *n.* One given the fortuitous opportunity to improve one's command of a foreign language (usually Arabic, these days) at a fraction of the Berlitz cost. One empowered by a withholding tax. *HOES-tij*, SHMOE-stij.

hostile (HAHS-t'l), *adj.* Warlike; liking war; forced to like war; (ab)normally antagonistic. *n.* A Native

American prior to the benevolent guidance of the Bureau of Indian Affairs (or, more likely, after). The author prefers the British *HAHS-ti-ul*, as it serves to distinguish the enemy from a flophouse or a morgue with a view.

humans (HYOO-munz), *n.* Hapless creatures born blind, loud, and naïve. Eyes open at about age forty. *YOO-muns* and *YOOS-tun* are typical Suburbiana, not to mention Texarkese.

hussy (HUH-ze, HUH-see), *n.* A woman who finds it difficult to choose a husband, and who, on occasion, may have to settle for her own. She is known to take a somewhat indelicate approach to social intercourse, leaving housewives suspicious of her virtue and envious of her ways.

ideologue (EYE-dee-uh-log), *n*. The kind of log that winds up on the court fire, if it doesn't regularly warm up to the king. *EYED-ee-uh-log* is cockeyed.

ideology (eye-dee-AHL-uh-jee), *n*. The study of the shortage of ideas, or the theory that all new ideas arise from sensationalism or sentimentalism, which was refuted by F. Scott Fitzgerald and Sir Winston

Churchill, who proved that most ideas arise from hallucinations caused by tobacco and good whiskey (with recent updates). According to Professor Nader, however, ideas from *both* sides of the aisle will carry a faint odor of formaldehyde well into the twenty-first century. *ID-ee-AHL-uh-jee* is reserved for alternative-pleasure seekers, wishful thinkers, and impulsive toe-tappers and teetotalers.

idyllic (eye-DIL-ik), *adj*. Of an idyll (*EYE-d'l*), or a short pastoral work evoking fondness in the reader for the pleasantness of the countryside. *The Grapes of Wrath*, an extended idyll of the 1930s, describes the charming lives of those close to the soil in Oklahoma and California, and how they make a new breast of it. *eye-DEAL-ik* is fabulously erroneous and too common among those who should know better.

ignoramus (ig-nuh-RAY-mus), *n*. Aside from anyone who does not purchase this darling dictionary, an ignoramus is generally a person who has managed to ignore everything but tabloids, talk shows, and Tinseltown, and who has taken Will Rogers's homely little statement to heart (but mostly to head): "Everybody's dumb about something." *ig-nuh-RAM-us*, no.

impious (IM-pe-us), *adj.* Not pious (*PIE-us*); overtly disrespectful toward God or, worse, the Church. In times past, severe punishment was exacted for the sin of impiety (*im-PIE-ih-tee*), but mostly in countries with no separation of Church and State (nor priest and altar boy). *im-PIE-us* is suspectly acceptable.

impotent (IM-puh-tunt), *adj.* Powerless or ineffective. Examples include the Securities and Exchange Commission, the Federal Aviation Agency, the Environmental Protection Agency, the United Nations, and the U.S. dollar. According to undisclosed sources, Pfizer's rumored new video game, "Hide the Weenie," will give new life to nonperformers, with the exception of the usual weenies in charge. *im-PO-tint* is as ineffective as it sounds.

inaugural (ih-NAW-gyuh-rul), *adj.* Of or relating to the inception of corruption. From the Latin "augur," an omen of corruption to come. *in-AW-gurl* is the usually corrupted form; *yu-GO-gurl* is OK in Oprahville (IL).

inchoate (in-KOE-ut), *adj.* Newly begun; a word applied obfuscatorially by sesquipedalians where such as "undisincipient" would do just as well. *in-koe-ATE* is acceptably incorrect.

incognito (in-kahg-NEE-toe, -tuh), *adj*. Disguised, or traveling under an assumed identity, such as a Dixiecrat in Republican clothing. It is said that Elvis, at the height of his popularity, could not stagger out of Graceland to fill an innocent prescription (or six) for fear of being mobbed, unless disguised as Dick Cheney. According to carefully leaked top-secret White House memos found in weekly editions of the *Globe* and *Tittle-Tattler* since 9/11/01, all "Elvis sightings" after "the King's" death are really Dick Cheney. Among other maskedly marvelous performers rumored to have been charged at one time or another with "assault on a potentially musical instrument" are Brian Warner, who travels undercover as Marilyn Manson and is thought to be the first black person in showbiz history to perform in "whiteface." *in-KAHG-nih-toe* is the author's preference, even though it's no longer NEET-o.

incredulous (in-KREJ-uh-lus), *adj*. Showing quizzical disbelief, especially after realizing that your computer's

Grammar Check does not recognize the word "incredulous." *in-KRED-uh-bull*, isn't it, Mr. Gates?

inquiry (in-CHOIR-ee), *n.* That which is convened after the fact, calling for the usual protocols and conventions of parliamentary debate; for example, "What the hell were you schmucks at the SEC doing all the time this was going on?" or "Prior to September 11, were you twerps at the CIA, NSA, FBI, INS, and Military Intelligence cooperating or just copulating?" *IN-kwuh-ree*, if you were copulating.

Iraq (ih-RAHK), *n.* Occupied zone in Southwestern Asia lacking security and intelligence but not pool tables and Ping-Pong. Approximately the size of California, Iraq has historically been ruled by those intent upon making a mess o' potamia. Voting apparatus and candidate selection similar to that of Florida. Domestic products consist mainly of moustache wax, moustache combs, moustache brushes, moustache trimmers (black market only), moustache implants, moustache shampoo, and The Moustache Club For Men (Only). Exports include dates, oil (when the pipelines are not being destroyed because of the lack of security and intelligence), and bluster. Capital is Baghdad. Former president is Saddam Hussein. Synonym is "Vietnam." *ee-RAK* is acceptable mediaspeak and *eye-RAK* is presidentially moronic.

irate (eye-RATE), *adj.* Piqued, pist. *EYE-rate* doesn't rate.

irony (EYE-ruh-nee), *n.* A type of expression employed by figureheads of speech who flatter too well. It is often directed at the legendary diligence of bureaucrats, the virtues of the middle class, the selflessness of politicians, and the modesty of televangelists. *EYE-urn-ee* and *IRON-ee* are cast in stone.

Isiah (eye-ZE-uh, ih-ZE-uh), *n.* Either this is an incorrect spelling of an eighth century B.C. Hebrew prophet's name (Isaiah), or it's a person having recently given the Byrd to Indiana. In any case, it cannot be slam-dunked as *eye-ZAY-uh.*

Israel (IZ-ree-ul, IZ-r'l), *n.* The smallest kid on the block, with the biggest punch. "MAH-vuh-lus!"

Jacques (ZHAHK). French given name. Can be pronounced as *JACK!*, in a pinch.

jaguar (JAG-wahr), *n*. A sleek beast said to be native to the rain forests of Coventry, England, where it is pronounced as *JAG-u-wahr*, or *JAG-u-ur*. Because of it (and Land Rover) having recently gone Stateside and the Germans having control over Rolls Royce, it is the opinion of the Shire that if Winston Churchill were alive today, he'd be turning over in his grave.

Janus (JAY-nus), *n*. A Roman god with the face of a human.

jerry-built / jury-rigged, *phr*.Confusable synonyms, meaning constructed with the care and quality found in tract houses or "motor hotels," especially the latter paper-walled palaces, which range from Seattle to San Diego and from Montreal to Montgomery, where the juries are said to be rigged with the greatest of care.

jousting (JOWST-ing), *n*. A feudal festivity that began with a tournament and ended with a tourni-*quet*, or two. Henry VIII is said to have lost his (wife's) head over it.

Judaism (JU-duh-iz'm), *n*. The religious, cultural, and social beliefs and practices of the Jews. For instance, all Jewish bars are operated by a guy by the name of Mitzvah; the expression "burning bush" currently serves equally as religious symbol and political objective; while the menus in Oak Park Chinese restaurants are printed in Hebrew. And that ain't just chopped liver, Oyving!

judiciary (juh-DISH-e-air-ee), *n.* The branch of government that hears cases and dispenses with justice. *juh-DISH-uh-re* warms the bench.

julienne (joo-le-EN), *n.* After Julien of Boston, French caterer. Originally a consommé containing sliced vegetables, as if from a paper shredder. *v.* To julienne, wherein one would first take a leek (okay, or a carrot), before washing and slicing the vegetable into matchstick thinness. *zhu-le-EN* also serves.

juncture (JUNK-chur), *n.* A particularly important time, state, or coming together (or, more often, apart) of things; a major cloverleaf in the freeway of life. *JUNK-shur* is the feminine.

Jung (YOOHNg), **Carl Gustav** (GOOHZ-tahv) (1875–1961). Swiss psychologist; contemporary of Freud; published important works concerning significance of dreams. Jung believed the ultimate human goal should be the achievement of harmony between the conscious (droll, natty, Londoners, New Yorkers, Torontons, Californians, etc.) and the unconscious (teenagers, retirees, etc.). *JOONG* and *JUNG* are dung.

junta (HOON-tuh), *n.* A group of plotters with designs on the group of plotters in power, some of whom are later consigned to their own plots as a reward for over-zealous plotting. *HUN-tuh* and *JUN-tuh* are also okay.

Juvenal (JOO-vuh-n'l), **Decimus Junius Juvenalis** (circa 60–140 A.D.). Savvy and savage satirist of early Roman excesses and champion of the underclass; the Lenny Bruce of antiquity. The roamin' excesses of today would've made him proud. *JOO-vuh-nawl* is incorrect. Synonym: George Carlin.

juvenile (JOO-vuh-nile), *adj.* Under-rage; the prefix of "delinquent." *JOO-vuh-nyl* is acceptable for most wardens. *n.* 1. A minor irritant appearing, typically, with head on backwards and forlorn visage, as if searching for a responsible adult. 2. The product of an arrested development (see "penalize").

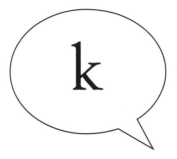

keelhauling (KEEL-hawl-ing) *n.* An unscheduled inspection of the underside of a ship at sea by one not particularly trained for the task.

ketchup (KEH-chup), *n.* The antisauce, according to French gastrotheology; a false sauce expected, by the editors of the Michelin Guide, to spread universal dyspepsia before the end of the world but finally to be conquered at the second coming of mayonnaise. *KAT-sup* and *KETS-up* are playing catch-up.

Khrushchev (KROOSH-chawf), **Nikita Sergeyevich** (1894–1971). Premier of Soviet Union (1958–64); sparring partner of JFK; pounded tables; led movement in 1960 to free journalist Helen Thomas from mediocre political assignments; had iron curtain-clad alibi for November 22, 1963, after consultation with Johnny Cochran; only person (aside from the author) ever barred from entrance to Disneyland.

kibbutz (kih-BOOTZ), *n*. Hebrew for a communal farm in Israel. Sometimes confused with "kibitz," less by Hebrews than non-, or *all the time* by the word-Smiths and Joneses of Fox News Live.

kibitz (KIH-buts), *v.i*. From the Yiddish "kibetsn," meaning to blather, meddle, obtrude, or generally annoy those trying diligently to cheat at cards, edit the putt count, etc. The word has reached new heights recently in the baseball broadcast booth, in lieu of the play-by-play.

kilometer (KILL-uh-me-tur), *n.* The basic international unit of linear travel by which the world drug crop, in kilograms (the basic international unit of weight), makes its way to the USA, surpassing French fries in popularity (and purity). *KILL-uh-SUCK-uh* is the basic unit of marketing. *kih-LAH-muh-tur* being the nickel bag.

kindergarten (KIN-dur-gahr-t'n), *n.* From the German for "garden of children," including weeds. A pregrade class in which ignoramuses bang at tambourines, screech wildly, and generally annoy the students. *KIN-e-gar-din* is current and eternal.

King of Pop, *phr.* Orville Redenbacher.

kismet (KIZ-met), *n.* The notion, beloved of the Occident, that there is romance in the fate of a fool. Also spelled "kismat." *kiz-MET*, for Yul Brynner fans.

KISS, *n.* Acronym for Keep It Simple Stupid. An expression originating in the business world, having gravitated to advertising, economics, and, of late, KISS has been fondly adopted by metal rock "music," where elderly performers are said to resemble a cross between a Mummers' Parade audition and a Navaho hoop dance contest, but not as loud. The group was slated to be the April 2005 centerfold for *Psychology Today* magazine, but they were rejected by the editors at the last minute as being too "straight" compared with the more youthful competition.

knuckle (NUH-k'l), *n*. A bony joint cast in the shape (and content) of a motorist's head.

Kublai Khan (KOO-bluh KAHN) (1215–1294). Mongol emperor; grandson of Genghis; liberal domestic agenda included national endowments for Khan artists and scientists; foreign policy in Southeast Asia similar to LBJ's. *KOO-bliy* and *KOO-blay* are somewhat okay.

kudos (KYOO-dahs), *n*. From the Greek "kydos," meaning acclaim or glory resulting from an achievement. Popular speakers, nudniks of news, and other tepid testimonians and polished media misnunciators—who will never be in danger of having their fingerprints lifted from a dictionary—

insist, in concert with their handlers, that this word is the plural of "kudo" (KOO-dough). And they are right—insofar as they and their brethren and sisteren are (ir)responsible for a thousand years of back-forming Greek-English language conversions, translations, and interpretations.

Ku Klux Klan (KOO KLUKS KLAN), *n*. An uneducable American anti-Black, anti-Brown, anti-Red, anti-Yellow, anti-Semitic, anti-Catholic, anti-Homosexual, anti-Intellectual, anti-cultural terrorist organization. The original uniform was a light-colored judicial robe and dunce cap. *KLOO-kluks* is the standard household mispronunciation, except in some precincts of Baton Rouge where it has been recently updated to Kongressman. Synonym: CIA.

Kuwait (koo-WAYT), *n*. Independent Arab sheikdom on the Persian Gulf. A British protectorate until 1961, it has been an Iraqi *protestorate* since 1756.

labor omnia vincit (LAY-bawr awm-nee-ah WING-kit). Latin phrase meaning "Vince will crush the scabs," loosely.

labyrinthine (lah-buh-RIN[t]-thun), *adj*. Like or similar to a labyrinth (*LAH-buh-rinth*), that is, a maze or other deliberately contrived confoundation such as the inner sanctum of a royal pyramid or the Medicare drug discount program.

Q:
So,
how
is Winton
Marsalis like an
Egyptian sarcophagus?
A: He has a TOOT-uncommon

lackadaisical (lah-kuh-DAY-zih-k'l), *v*. To be short a daisical. It is not certain how many daisicals are currently required for proper daisical balance; however, according to Dr. Vivilore Kapoosta, spokesperson for the Federal Daisical Task Force, the number varies among generations, occupations, and professions, and those who lack one are said to be quite apparent even to the untrained eye or ear, as they attack their duties at the bureaus, agencies, departments, 911 phone banks, and associated institutions. Obfuscators and obstructionists are those who are *two* under the daisical ideal. *LAX-uh-DAY-zih-k'l*, popularly.

Lackawanna, *n*. Absence of desire.

laissez-faire (leh-say-FAIR). French for "let them do what they will." Not a Boomer child-raising principle, but an expression associated with economic pursuits wherein regulative government busybodies are not so busy. The phrase has also been applied, from time to time, to the highness of the judicial hand and, indeed, to His Highness, the judge, Himself. Mispronunciation occurs generally as *LAY-ZAY-FAIR*.

Lao-tse (LAOUD-ZUH) (circa sixth century B.C.). Historically questionable founder of Taoism (*DAOU-ih-z'm*), a Chinese religion espousing rather fantastic, far-fetched, and outlandish principles, including the abjuration of striving, the cultivation of kindness, a noncompetitive economy, honest hearing-aid salesmen, and a tasteful hairdo for Donald Trump. *LOU-TSAY* and *TOW-ih-s'm* are the usual clinkers.

lapis lazuli (lap-us-LAY-zuh-lee), *n*. A nontransparent, sky-blue semiprecious stone, purchased by females for adornment and by (transparent) males for atonement. *LAZ-yoo-lee*, usually.

largesse or **largess** (lahr-ZHES), *n*. Formerly, generosity; currently, the accusation of generosity, generally well defended. Accentual error is most common, followed by the usual suffixial indiscretions, as in "Your largesse is legend, madame."

laryngitis (lair-un-JI-tus), *n*. In humans, an insufficiently frequent loss of gossip, lip service, or doublespeak; caused by the swelling of the membrane lying posterior to the angle formed by the mouth. *LAHR-in-JI-tus*, in anterior tongues.

larynx (LAIR-inks), *n*. The structure at the upper end of the human trachea (*TRAY-ke-uh*) containing the organ of vocal incontinence and nonelectronic noise. One of the most frequently mispronounced words, it is commonly heard as *LAHR-niks*, both clinically and otherwise. Plural is "larynges" (*luh-RIN-jeez*).

lasso (LAH-so), *n*. A lariat or rope, traditionally with a saddle horn at one end and a horse thief at the other. Secondary uses do exist. *lass-OOH* is what was heard in the '40s, when a quarter would buy it all at the RKO and J. D. Salinger began contemplating his novel.

lawyer (LAW-yur), *n.* One whose training in the law commonly does not hinder him in practice. Pronunciation varies regionally; that is, from side to side of the courtroom or the jailhouse. Incorrect pronunciation of this word can be quite amusing, to say the least. Synonym is "accountant."

Le Creuset (luh kru-ZAY), *phr.* French for "Do not drop on toe!" The logo of a French manufacturer of barbells that they are pleased to call cookware. *Lay kru-ZET*, non!

lederhosen (LAY-dur-hose-un), *n.* German for "leather pants." Specifically, short leather pants, traditionally worn with an Alpine hat, suspenders, and a Bavarian beer belly. Not *LEE-dur-hose-un*.

leg (LEHG), *n.* The part of the drug-friendly human anatomy that's "pulled" more often than given an "up." "*LAYG!*" is the variant heard by novice infantrymen who are five jumps short, the speaker's vocabulary remaining about three quarts low.

legume (LEH-gyoom), *n.* Any plant (with a memory) of the *leguminosae* family (let me pronounce that for you: *FAM-uh-lee*), including peas, beans, etc., regularly consumed by those who throw caution to the winds. *lih*-GOOM and *lih*-GYOOM being the alternates.

Leif (LAYV), *n.* As in Leif Ericsson, part of the coalition of Christopher Columbus, Sir Francis Drake, Al Gore, and Hagar the Horrible claiming credit for discovering America. That's *LIFE*, to some.

leisure (LEE-zhur), *n.* A time of inactivity: for a bureaucrat, between the hours of 9 A.M. and 5 P.M.; for a politician, between reelection campaigns; for a student, between the ages of four and twenty-two. *LEZH-ur* is the preference of Connecticut Yankees in federal court.

Leno (LEN-o), **Jay** (1950–). Two under Paar.

Leroux (luh-ROOH), **Gaston** (1868–1927). French writer and author of popular 1894 do-it-yourself pamphlet entitled *How to Build a Five-Manual Pipe Organ in a Paris Sewer Using Only Spare Parts from a Bicycle.*

Later retitled *The Phantom of the Opera*. His name is seldom if ever mentioned in playbills or movie credits, possibly violating the laws of plagiarism but most certainly pooh-poohing the requirements of simple courtesy and respect, not to mention insulting the Lance Armstrong crowd.

l'etat c'est moi (lay-TAH say MWAH). French phrase reputedly from Louis XIV, meaning, basically, "I am the state," or, a bit closer to the throne, "If the Englishman doesn't drop the 'Cat-Horse' crap, I'll have his freaking head."

lever (LEH-vur), *n*. One of the classic simple machines, the others being the wheel and the screw. The lever consists of a bar and a fulcrum for lifting, prying, etc.; as distinguished from a political machine, where a wheel with enough leverage is able to screw the public admirably. *LEE-vur* being the Pronunciation Ordinaire.

liability (lie-uh-BIL-uh-tee), *n*. The most popular kind of ability. *lie-BIL-uh-tee* passes.

liaison (LEE-uh-zahn, lee-AY-zahn), *n*. Communication (or a communicator) for the establishment of mutual cooperation between, say, departments of a federal government, as in the newly established American Secretary of Homeland Security, who will act as liaison between the Border Patrol, Coast Guard, and U.S. Customs Service. This was designed to make the three agencies just as successful in the apprehension of terrorists as they are in the interdicting of illegal drugs at the beloved boundaries, ports, and frontiers.

liberal (LIH-brul, LIH-buh-rul), *n*. Half of the ruling dynasty of America, the other half being the conservative. Both halves are connected at the *lip* by the glue of bluster. *adj*. Free-thinking, open-minded. The author is not aware of the existence, in the USA, of a "Conservative Arts" college, at least not in name. Nor the "Religious Left."

libido (luh-BE-doe, LIH-buh-doe), *n*. Psychic or sexual energy derived from primitive pharmaceutical urges, which is controlled commonly by giving in to them. The libido was uncovered by Freud and hasn't had a stitch on since.

lichen (LIY-kun), *n.* A plant of the algae-fungi persuasion, sometimes known to adorn a Southern California salad plate. It is erroneously associated with arctic regions.

licorice (LIH-kuh-rish), *n.* Modern lexicons are pleased to list *LIH-kuh-rish* as the first acceptable pronunciation, which serves to confuse "licorice" with "lickerish," or "liquorish," both meaning sensuous to the point of debauchery. Who are whee! to argue.

lingerie (lahn-juh-RAY), *n.* Ladies' *underies*, unless you're Madonna, then it's ladies' *overies*. *lahn-zhuh-RAY*, optionally, of corset.

liposuction (LIH-puh-suk-shun), *n.* A relatively new surgery involving the "vacuuming" of fat from the torso and thighs of the morbidly obese (although in the greater Potomac area—and some talk show venues—it is seen as a cranial procedure). *LIP-o-suk-shun* is incorrect, but instructive.

liqueur (lih-KUR), *n.* A slightly viscous, flavored liquor; the thinking man's cough syrup. *lih-KYOOR* is said to be acceptable at *Gourmet* magazine's piano bar.

literati (lih-tuh-RAH-tee), *n*. From the Latin, plural of "literatus" (lih-tuh-RAH-tus), men of letters, and now also women, with the advent of the Equal Writes Amendment. *lih-tuh-RAW-tee* is naughty.

literature (LIH-tuh-ruh-choor), *n*. The body of imaginative writings, including spleen; as distinguished from, say, modern reportage and other novelle. Literature was once taught and superficially learned in the USA, but was replaced in 1982 with seminars on the First Amendment rights of the Grateful Dead and the accessibility of "page-turners" to those addicted to Cliffs Notes. *LIT-ih-chur* is a presidential favorite, while the dandy *LIH-trih-tyoor* is plainly cotillionesque.

London (LUHN-duhn). Capital of England. Primary residence, seat of office, and headquarters of democratic heads of Islamic regimes and Muslim dictators of Mideastern democracies. Synonyms: Paris; Washington, D.C.

longevity (lahn-JEV-uh-tee), *n*. Agedliness. Current medical guesswork suggests that longevity is largely a gene-driven condition fraught with wrinkles, bad breath, and retirement—an ugliness that popular performers and other alternative lifestylists are mysteriously able to nip in the bud. (Carbon dating of members of the House Judiciary Committee and the Senate Foreign Relations Committee was inconclusive at this time.) *lawng-JEV-uh-tee* is faulty.

longshoremen, *n.* A pier group.

Los Angeles (laws-AN-juh-luhs). Largest city in California, characterized by Extreme Reverend Skip "Chip" Plume as *A Study in Gray & Brown, with Car Chases.* Alternate pronunciation is *ELLAY,* said with a sneer by those who can't afford to live there.

Louisville (LOO-ih-v'l), *n.* Bourbon city in Kentucky. Locals and wanna-be "colonels" will reduce this to one and a half syllables on request.

Louvre (LOO-vruh, LOOV), *n.* A French tourist facility of no interest to Americans, as it lacks a drive-thru window and a water slide. According to Parisites, Brits are able to jog through it in about twenty-two minutes (including lunch).

Love (LUHHV), *n.* Antidisenchantmentarianism.

Luciano (loo-CHAHN-o). As in Pavarotti. Off the Continent, the great tenor's name is invariably pronounced as *loo-see-AN-o*. As for "Pavarotti," arts-channel fund-raisers, classical disk jockeys, museum-keepers, and other hacks are not embarrassed to reduce that to *pav-uh-RAH-de*. Give the man a *little* respect.

lucubration (loo-kyuh-BRAY-shun), *n*. Word or thought processing done at night or by artifice-ial light; nocturnal emissions of a literary nature; turgid (and, on occasion, suspect) scholarship bathed in the glow of pedantry, to the antonymity of this author's distinguished, erudite, and underrated masterwork. *lyoo-kyuh-BRAY-shun* is bray-acceptable.

lugubrious (luh-GOO-bre-us), *adj*. Ridiculously or affectedly grief-stricken; melodramatically sad; as might be a B-movie actor, a deep-discount mortician, a convention of Highland Park hookers, or a trouper from the Consumer Product Safety Commission. Crocodile tears shed by Republican presidents over workers victimized by multinational corporate thugs are also covered under this heading. *luh-GUB-re-us*, not.

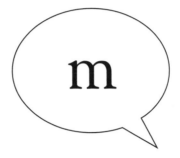

macabre (muh-KAHB), *adj*. Ghastly, gruesome, or grotesque, as in *danse macabre*, or the other "danses" (with wolves, for instance). Dickens's always optimistic Mr. Micawber fits nicely into this category.

macaw (muh-KAW), *n*. Loudmouthed, showy parrots of tropical America. Very often heads of state of Central and South American countries give visiting dignitaries the bird as *toucans* of their esteem. *MAY-kaw* is less correct.

machete (muh-SHEH-tee), *n*. A large, heavy, long-bladed knife, common in Cuba, Jamaica, Rwanda, the Ivory Coast, etc., and which, in an emergency, can also be used to cut sugar cane. *match-ETT-ee* and *muh-CHET-ee* can't hack it.

machismo (mah-CHEEZ-mo), *n*. Overstated, overrated masculinity in men. In other words, the kind of CHEEZ you'd expect from the locker room, the barroom, the playing fields of Eton, and the Chevy lowrider. The emergency room is also known as a receptacle of *mah-CHEEZ-e-ness*, especially during Super Bowl week, when, statistically, more assaults on machismo mamas take place than at any other time of the year. Overstated, overrated masculinity in women is called "bodybuilding." But at least their masculinity smells a little better. *mah-KEEZ-mo*, *muh-KEEZ-mo*, *mah-KIZ-mo*, and *muh-CHIZ-mo* are all testosterone-approved.

madam (MAH-dum), *n.* The palindromic title of the mistress of a household; in certain other houses, a woman with a Ph.D. in carnal knowledge. *muh-DAM* is correct only in French houses, damnit!

mademoiselle (mad-mwuh-ZELL), *n.* An unmarried French woman or girl (as if that makes any difference). Give it up for the French!

magnate (MAG-nayt), *n.* A self-made cheat, rather than a dissipated inheritor. A corporate executive who would never: 1. Mislead shareholders; 2. Embezzle from the pension fund; 3. Accept bonuses during down times; 4. Lie like hell to the SEC. Magnatic personality, always.

Malathion (mah-luh-THIGH-un), *n.* A feel-good insecticide (except for the insects). *muh-LAY-thee-ahn* is just a bit more toxic and begs the question: "Is that your final ant, sir?"

malcontent (mal-kun-TENT), *n.* One whose disenchantment with the official corruption has led him to the urging-on of the people's. The pronunciation *mal-KAHN-tent* is reserved for "sequel" movies and novels, tabloids, *Rolling Stone*, and jars of pickled pigs' knuckles.

malefactor (MAL-uh-fak-tur), *n.* Evildoer. Female-factor, or malefactress, has recently enjoyed a box-office vogue. *MAIL-fak-tur* often goes postal.

malted (MAWLT-ed), *n.* A shake's peer.

Malthusian (mal-THOO-zhun), *adj.* Of or about Thomas Robert Malthus (1766–1834), who theorized that widespread humans would eventually screw themselves off the earth on an empty stomach. He did not take into account, however, the advent of the "corn belt," the air-conditioned tractor, the subsidy fat cats, and the mass production of synthetic foods such as soy curd, granola bars, and Big Max.

Maori (MAH-o-ree), *n.* A member of a Polynesian people native to New Zealand; an Old Zealander. *may-ORR-ee* and *may-ORR-i* will arouse ire on the high seas.

Mao Tse-tung (MAH-o [d]zuh-DOONG). Hunanese peasant having made it big in the city. Born 1893; immortal, by law. Founder of People's Republic of China and the 30 x 40 foot weatherproof portrait. *MOW say-TUNG* will cause raised eyebrows and a shrug when you go there to visit the American Balance of Trade Hall of Fame.

maraschino (mair-uh-SKEE-no), *n.* A marinated cherry inhabiting a mixed drink that will soon inhabit a marinated drinker. *mair-uh-SHEE-no* is much easier to slur when you're marinated.

marchioness (MAR-shuh-nus), *n.* Here's an everyday word. She is the wife of a marquis (*MAR-kwus*), the member of an English upper household who cleans up after the servants. *MAR-che-uh-NESS* and *mar-KEE* are incorrect, the latter unless you are in a French brothel or at a Lincoln-Mercury dealership in Sun City.

Marquis de Sade (SAHD), *pn.* The man who would be *kink*.

m

Marseilles (mar-SAY), *n.* Picturesque Mediterranean seaport containing a French Quarter and an Arab Quarter. (It's not certain who's living in the other half of town.)

masonry (MAY-s'n-ree), *n.* The work of masons. Amateurish compared to the stonewalling that goes on among those of the parliamentary persuasion. *MAY-s'n-air-ee,* in aisle 9 at Home Depot.

mathematics (math-MAT-iks), *n.* Branch of science dealing with numbers, which don't lie, and their relationships with CPAs, CFOs, and CEOs, who do. *math-uh-MAT-iks* seems to be the favored coin of longer-winded accounting firms whose balance sheets remain in oh-so-fretful disarray and are being targeted, reportedly, by the Senate Select Committee for Truth and Corporate Crap in Math, headed by the rather suspiciously insufficiently suspicious Senator Dodd.

mature (muh-TOOR), *adj.* Responsible; legally entitled to pornography, beer, and road rage. *v.* To become ripe for the picking or the ripping (off). *muh-TYOOR* and *muh-CHOOR* are the dated voicings used mainly by those who've never dated.

Maupassant (mo-puh-SAWN[t]), **Guy de** (GHEE duh) (1850–93). Prolific writer of novels and short stories, the worst of which gained great popularity. A public servant, he went mad in 1891. What a Guy! All together now: Henri (*aw-RE*) Rene (*ruh-NAY*) Albert (*all-BEAR*) Guy (*GHEE*) de (*duh*) Maupassant (*mo-puh-SAWN[t]*).

Mauve (MAWV), *n*. The color purple, as the mallow in the marsh that Man insists is white. MOEV is off-color.

McCarthyism, *n*. A Red *hearing*.

McLean (muh-KLANE), *n*. A city in Virginia bordering on criminal negligence, malfeasance, and capital offenses. *mik-LEEN* also violates.

mea culpa (may-uh KUL-puh). Latin for "My bad!" Today, a rare expression, especially among North Americans and other beneficiaries of twenty-first-century advances in self-righteousness genetics and innocence entitlements.

m

medieval (mee-DEE-vul), *adj*. Said of backward feudal domains where, sooner or later, the people will demand paved streets, legitimate elections, and the suppression of warlords, such as in Kabul, Mogadishu, Detroit, etc. *mih-DEE-vul* and *meh-dee-E-vul* are okay constructs, too.

medium rare, *phr*. A half-baked notion proposed by naïve waiters.

mellifluous (meh-LIF-fluh-wus), *adj*. Sweetly flowing, suchlike Amadeus Mozart, John Keats, Jack Daniels, etc. From "mellow," meaning "to become sweet with age," as with balsamic vinegar or fine Port; as distinguished from retirees, cocker spaniels, doones*berries*, etc. *muh-LIH-fuh-lus* is the anti-sweet.

melodic (muh-LAH-dik), *adj*. Lacking the character of modern music, poetry, speech; unpleasant to the tin ear. *mel-LO-dik*, in the usual low places.

memento (muh-MEN-toe), *n*. An easily mispronounced word (as *mo-MEN-toe*) by legitimate citizens, as well as actors (the great Sidney Greenstreet uttered it to Bogart in *The Maltese Falcon*), curators, souvenir-shop proprietors, and those sporting "I'd Rather Be . . ." bumper stickers.

memorabilia (meh-muh-ruh-BIH-lee-uh), *n*. Collections of symbolic doo-dads, gewgaws, and gimcracks. Memorabilia are jealously protected by the memorabilious (collectors and curators), evoking, on occasion, weepiness; as distinguished from "antiques" and "works of the masters," or those items in the inventory of "brokers" and others possessed of a waning fascination with honesty. ("Inventors" are called in regularly to plan the flotsam of the future.) *meh-muh-ruh-BEE-lee-uh* is correct only for bottle-cap and beer-can aficionados.

menstruation (men-stru-WAY-shun), *n*. An event occurring among female primates beginning at puberty. The lemur mother is said to be the first among the order to care enough to prepare offspring for the approach of the event, followed by the orangutan, chimpanzee, gorilla, and tarsier. *men-STRAY-shun* is the come-lately, all too commonly.

mentor (MEN-tur), *n*. An adviser. An especially *effective* adviser when carrying the prefix "tor." *MEN-tor* and *MEN-tawr* are commonplace.

Messianic E-mail, *phr*. A Godsend.

miasma (my-AZ-muh), *n*. A vapor arising from decaying animal and/or plant material, as that from swamps, retirees, the works of Karl Marx, the sneakers of a twelve-year-old, etc. (The works of *Julius* Marx, however, are ever fresh and enduring.) *me-AZ-muh* is incorrect, now and again.

midget (MIH-jut), *n*. Position occupied between upperget and lowerget.

Midwest (mid-WEST), *n*. There is usually not a pronunciation problem here—except, of course, among those in twelve-step Game Boy recovery, the Cliff-Dwellers of Charlotte, the Lang-wedge clans of Quebec, Bronx cheerleaders, and lifetime subscribers to *Soldier of Fortune* magazine. *MIDLANDS* would be correcter.

minuscule (MIH-nus-kyool), *adj.* Tiny; minute. Originally, a type of small-lettered medieval script— fine print—said to have gained favor among merchants of the day who sold horses and/or suits of armor with a warranty and a Sir charge. In the USA, closest synonym is "deceptive and fraudulent, but legal." Frequently misspelled as "miniscule" and mispronounced accordingly.

mirror (MIHR-ur), *n.* An evil engine of the West, which, when gazed upon with regularity, is said to rob one's spirit and steal one's youth. The modern mirror was invented in 1891 by Dr. D. R. N. Gray, a London cosmetic surgeon who was said to have had a nodding acquaintance with the devil. *MEER* is current coin of the linguistically penniless and the monosyllabically possessed. Note: From the manner in which members of the over-sixty-five crowd (mostly male) choose to appear in public, it is to be deduced that mirrors may not exist in the retirement community at all.

m

mischievous (MIS-chuh-vus), *adj.* Darkly playful. Not *all* trial lawyers and network news anchors pronounce it as *mis-CHEE-vee-us*.

missile (MIH-sul), *n.* The canny Brits, in order to distinguish a bomb from a Catholic annual report (or maybe not), pronounce this as *MISS-isle*. The Yanks, who are undistinguished, pronounce both as *MIH-sul*.

Missouri (miss-OOH-ree), *n.* Name of a midland American state containing the city of St. Louis, a metropolis having recently taken on some airs and rather snobbish ways as it has unceremoniously dethroned Detroit as "the most dangerous city in the U.S." This name is almost never pronounced properly and stands either at *mih-ZUR-uh* (for residents) or *mih-ZOOR-ee* (for noblessent or affected tourists). *MIZZ-uh-ree* is never correct, but often appropriate.

Monticello (mahn-tuh-SELL-o), *n.* The estate of Thomas Jefferson—statesman, architect, philosopher, and general fool-arounder. No one is home. *mahn-tuh-CHEL-o* is incorrect, except when referring to a fiddle sized between a Montiviola and a Monti-doublebass.

Moore (MOAR, MORE). Surname of a long line of geniuses, including an Archibald, an Archie, a

Marianne, a Hannah, three Thomases, and not enough Michaels.

moral majority. *phr.* A plurality of sinners who sit on the right hand of God, the Father Allwhitey.

mortar and pestle (MORE-tur and PEH-sul), *n.* The barber pole of the druggist; the national flag of Colombia. In North America, druggists of suspect accreditation are symbolized by the mortar and pistol; in South America and Afghanistan, the 85-mm mortar and pistol. *PEST-ul* is incorrect.

Moscow (MAHS-kow). A town in northwestern Idaho; and, oh yes, the former *capital* of Cuba. *MAHS-ko* sets weller with mediaennes.

Mousquetaires (moo-skuh-TARS), *n.* French musketeers, primarily noted for not carrying muskets. As distinguished from Mouseketeers, who are shorter, if you don't count the ears.

moustache (muh-STASH), *n.* See "mustache," if you must.

m

mouth, *n.* A gaping hole in the defences of propriety.

mustache (MUSS-tash), *n.* An unsightly lippal adornment, primarily of men, that has recently given way to the unsightly Van Dyke, or "goatee," as the all-you-can-eat crowd, field reporters, and camo boys are wont to say. STASH!

m

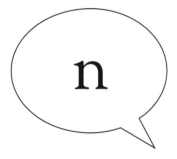

nadir (NAY-dur), *n*. From the Arabic "nazir," meaning "opposite" (of zenith). Ground zero; bottom; the point at which an entity cannot sink any lower, with the possible exception of talk radio, rap "lyrics," competitive eating, the *Anna Nicole Show*, etc.

naïve (nah-EEV), *adj*. Confident that the news story "coming up next" will come up next or that the "4-Wheel Brake Special For $99!" will cost $99. Trustful of telemarketers, developers, realtors, stock analysts, hair clubs, diet plans, wrinkle creams, pension-fund custodians, "friendly" pit bulls, or any American who says that he knows what's going on in the Middle East. That's just plain *ny-EEV!*

naïvete (nah-eev-TAY), *n.* A property of those who believe that a belt with a battery will turn a beer belly into a washboard; that a magnet will cure a migraine; that a pill will fill your bra; that there *is* a War on Drugs; that your "unlisted" phone number is unavailable; that "With this plan you will retire at forty"; or that an even number of socks will come out in the dryer. *ny-EEV-ih-tee,* no.

nanometer (NA-nuh-me-tur), *n.* One billionth of a meter, or the size of a pinhead and its usual escorts: the airhead, the (hip)hop-head, and other of the congenitally boggleminded. Ten nanometers are equal to an angstrom, or the length and breadth of human understanding, as determined by network news executives. *nan-AHM-uh-tur* is short.

nanosecond (NA-nuh-seh-kund), *n.* The attention span of a "good ole boy" or a "nice li'l girl"; the length of time a Palestinian cease-fire holds. *NAN-o*, no-no.

Narcissus (nar-SIS-us), *n.* Greek mythological figure whose woeful lack of personal standards was ultimately reflected in his choice of a lover. A Boomer hero. *NAR-sis-sis*, erroneous is.

nauseate (NAW-zhe-ate), *v.t.* To cause to contemplate butter substitutes, bacon alternatives, eight-dollar tequila, or a life without chili-dogs; followed by *Fear Factor*, the public airing of 911 calls, and those who cavort in public in their underwear. *NAW-see-ate* is unsightly.

nauseous (NAW-shus, NAW-ze-us), *adj.* Causing nausea (NAW-zee-uh), a vomitus malaise accompanying the natural systemic rejection to health foods, soap operas, Ms. Senior pageants, rapsters, recruiters, freebooters, sloganeers, proselytizers, paid programming, and Old Spice.

Nazis (NAHT-sees), *n*. A party thrown by Adolf Hitler and crashed by Dwight D. Eisenhower. General A. C. McAuliffe brought the "Nuts!" during the 101st Airborne's 1944 yuletide visit to Field Marshal von Rundstedt, who ultimately shrank from the caliber of gifts delivered by General Patton. The British *NAH-zees* is extremely attractive as it requires just the right amount of sneer.

Neanderthal (ne-AN-dur-tawl), *adj*. Of a type of primitive man whose remains were discovered in the Neander valley of Germany. DNA extracted from its fossilized feces shows a remarkable resemblance to brain matter of today's road-ragers, desert runners, tank-toppers, alarmists, enviro-terrorists, gang-bangers, and lounge lizards.

negotiate (nih-GO-she-ate), *v.i.* To cease ineffective hostilities and commence effective equivocation. *v.t.* To arrive at a price, preferably in a bulldozer. *nih-GO-see-ate* is the pronunciation of field reporters, the tongue-tied, and others not allowed in the studio.

Nevada (nuh-VAH-duh), *n*. U.S. state and home of the infamous Las Vegas (*loss VAY-gus*), which is

Spanish for "Leave your testicles at the door on the way out." Vegas is the religionous capital of the Western hemisphere and where the relics of Occidentalism are stored: the Shroud of Tourin' and the Ark of the Condiment. Tenets require worshipers to make a pilgrimage to "VAY-gis" at least once or thrice a year for seven days and eleven nights. After pawnbrokering, payday lending, self-abuse therapy, and bankruptcy counseling, gambling ("gaming") is said to be the chief industry. Winners' photos are displayed on a 3 x 5 card at the city limits on the way out of town. Because of its massive lighting displays, Las Vegas is reportedly the only object visible to the naked eye at night from the international space station, aside from Jimmy Carter's teeth, that is.

New Orleans (noo-AWR-lee-unz, NAW-lunz). Scenic Louisiana city on the Mississippi (or *in* the Mississippi, depending on the season) and home to Mardi Gras, which is French for "Show your tits!" *noo-awr-LEENZ* is perky but imperfect.

niche (NITCH), *n.* From the French "nicher," meaning "to nest." A deserving place; a nook; an appropriate position, unless it was gained by fraud, or not. President

George W. Bush was rumored to have pronounced it as *NICK-ey*, at a briefing in 2002. He was then roundly criticized by the press for not saying *NEESH*.

nicotine (NIH-kuh-teen), *n*. In the USA, an unfashionable alkaloid believed to be the cause of the "Non-Smoking Area" sign and other secondhand commercial grammar. (The author quit smoking cold turkey and went back to cigarettes.) It is also rumored to be the source of ongoing controversy between Big Tobacco and Big Fed (in bed), with regard to (black) market share, while Big Drug, Big Cola, Big Gin, Big Caffeine, and Big Carb are said to be waiting in the wings to pick up the pieces.

nirvana (nir-VAH-nuh), *n*. A state of indescribable bliss reserved for the souls of Buddhists, who, since the seventh century B.C., have not bothered to describe it. It has been variously interpreted by Western theologians as equivalent to driving through rush-hour traffic without incident, retaining an attorney or physician who will return your phone calls, knowing which of the #1 college football teams is #1, or figuring out the chronology of *Star Wars*. *nur-VAH-nuh* is okay, too.

Nisei (nee-SAY), *n.* Japanese for "second generation." A Japanese-American born of immigrant parents and educated in the U.S.—generally looked down on by literate grandparents. *Nee-say* is not nice, see!

Nitrous oxide, *n.* A brew ha-ha.

Nobel (no-BELL), **Alfred** (1833–1896). Inventor of dynamite. The latest dynamite being the awarding of the Nobel Peace Prize to Jimmy Carter who, in the years following his presidency, furthered "the cause" by monitoring social and electoral processes in third-world venues such as Djibouti and Broward County. *NO-bull* is incorrect but has some possibilities.

nonagenarian (no-nuh-juh-NAIR-e-un), *adj.* Between ninety and a hundred years of age. The U.S. state containing the most nonagenarians is Minnesota, no doubt because of the salubrious environment. (Cryonics is reportedly no longer practiced there because of the stiff competition from the weather.) Southern California, now, has the highest population of people who don't age at all, a chronological phenomenon that stymied even Einstein and Rod Serling but which explains why the author's age is slowly but surely catching up to Liz Taylor's, for example.

nonpareil (nahn-puh-RELL), *adj*. Peerless; unrivaled; unequaled (in a lexiconical sense); a "perfect 10" (for the redundunce crowd). *NAHN-puh-REEL* and *nahn-PAIR-e-ul* are *unrell*.

"No problem," *phr*. The expression "you're welcome" (theoretically following "thank you") has evidently gone the way of the ground sloth, civility, and clean-shaven Balkan women. If (unconscious) rudeness is "in," "no problem" is its escort.

Nostradamus (nahs-truh-DAH-mus), **Michel de Notredame** (1503–66). Brilliant French physician-turned-astrologer (malpractice insurance must've been going through the roof then, too). His "predictions," written in the form of cryptic quatrains, have been the source of some of the most astute guesswork since researchers started trying to figure out the Origin of Species and the Indecency of Man. *nahs-truh-DAME-us* is upon us.

nubile (NOO-bile), *adj*. Said of young women exhibiting certain physical characteristics that tend to give rise to proposals, and such. *NOO-b'l* is no bull, neither!

nuclear (NOO-klee-ur), *adj*. Just as "realtor" remains constant and unyielding among the speak-lazy as *REE-luh-tur*, so is "nuclear" steadfastly prized within their ranks as *NOO-kyuh-lur*. Mr. Carville insists upon *NUK-yuh-lur*, on *Crossfire*, giving him something in common (horrors!) with W (*NOOK-uh-lur*) on *Press Conference Live*.

nuncupative (NUNG-kyoo-pay-tiv), *adj*. Oral, as opposed to badly written. Legal term used in reference to whimsical wills and imperishable probate, or the naming, as heir, of the least offensive vulture hovering over the bed of the soon-to-be deceased. *nun-KOOP-puh-tiv* for the joint account frauds.

nuptial(s) (NUP-chuhl, NUP-shuhl), *adj*. In the USA, descriptive of the second step toward divorce. The first step being prenuptial, the last postnuptial, or the awarding of trophies (in case the first step was

n

overlooked), the ex-husband's testicles and assets going to an attorney and the attorney's mistress (the ex-husband's ex-wife), or vice versa. *NUP-chew-uhl* is not palatable.

n

oatmeal, *n. Gruel* and unusual punishment.

obelisk (AH-buh-lisk), *n.* An erect structure based on a phallusy, and symbolic, typically, of a tyrant's screwing of the people. Washington's is monumental. *OOH-buh-lisk* is short.

oblate (AH-blate), *adj.* Geometrically round in the

middle, flattened at the poles, as in "oblate spheroid," which is the shape of the planet Earth, a triple cheeseburger, or a standard consumer, according to the CDC (Conspiracy of Dietary Charlatans). *OH-blate* is oh-so-wrong.

obligatory (uh-BLIH-guh-tore-ee), *adj.* Necessary; mandatory; required, as in "prior to 1971 and 'wall of sound' technology, popular musicians were required to have a voice and/or actually be able to play a musical instrument."

O

obsequious (ub-SEE-kwee-us), *adj.* Fawning, subservient, reverent, affectedly humble, etc. in the presence of royalty, that is, anyone charging $25 to autograph a baseball, basketball, football. (The *author* is fawning, subservient, reverent, etc., in the presence of royal*ties*.) *ahb-ZEK-we-us*, no.

oncologist (ahn-KAWL-uh-jist), *n.* A "rad" sawbones whose patients tend to give him glowing reviews.

onerous (AH-nuh-rus), *adj.* Legally obliged to do the right thing (if the judge feels like it). *OWE-nuh-rus* is acceptable and often appropriate.

one-upmanship, *n.* Conversation. This expression, like "brink(s)manship," is usually burdened with an extra "s." One-upmanship is a heated exchange of remarks (commonly among men), the object of which is to get in the last word, thus becoming "one up"; as distinguished from "repartee" in that it lacks the advantage of wit. (Women and mothers-in-law instinctively pooh-pooh one-upmanship as being merely so much trifling by amateurs.)

opera (AH-puh-ruh, AH-pruh), *n.* Lust, murder, and intrigue on the high Cs.

ophthalmologist (ahf-thuhl-MAH-luh-jist), *n.* A "sick-eye-atrist," or one who treats the primary organ of gawking, according to Dr. Isaac Dahktor, celebrated inventor of the talking tire pressure gauge for the legally blind. Next to the pharmacist and the editor of the complaint column, the busiest guy in West Palm Beach. *Ahp-thuh-MAH-luh-jist* is seeing its way clear currently.

optimist (AHP-tuh-mist), *n.* One who sees only half of TV programming as *empty.* As distinguished from the pessimist, who sees the optimist as *full* of crap.

opulence (AH-pyuh-lun[t]s), *n*. Sumptuous trappings; chichi accouterments. Traditionally a result of the moneyed elite's disdain for good taste.

orangutan (uh-RANG-uh-tang), *n*. Malay for "man of the forest." A solitary, manlike ape of Borneo and Sumatra, with reddish-brown shaggy hair and very long arms (left-handed, reportedly). An intelligent, teachable beast, it is said to prefer Oscar Wilde, Tom Wolfe, the Algonquin Round Table, and Hagar the Horrible over *Who Moved My Cheese?*, celebrity memoirs, National Safety Council bulletins, and the Op-Ed page. *o-RANG-uh-tang* and *uh-RANG-uh-tan*, slopshiddedly.

ordnance (AWRD-nun[t]s), *n*. Military weaponry. As distinguished from "ordinance," or civil weaponry. Both conform to the law of supply and The Man.

Oregon. Northwestern U.S. state and river. Capital: Salem. Chief crop: oregano. *AWR-ih-gun* is the pronunciation of choice of indentured natives and indicted inlanders, while *AWR-uh-gahn* identifies coastal Califoreignians, DEA and FBI SWAT teams, and illegal importers of oregano.

origami (awr-uh-GAH-me), *n.* The Japanese art of folding paper into decorative shapes. Retirees and those on "fixed incomes" are masters of it, being able to artfully fold a one-dollar bill to resemble a four-dollar tip for a $60 check. *or-ih-GAME-ee* is gamey.

Ouija (WEE-juh), *trademark.* A popular board game used to transmit messages from the spirits, usually 100 proof. In which case *WEE-JEE* works.

outré (ooh-TRAY), *adj.* Bizarre, dotty, far-out, outlandish, unheard of, as in Shaquille O'Neal making two free throws in a row, a courteous Chicago motorist, a New Ager filling a prescription, a school bus *not* stopped on railroad tracks, an MTV Video Music Awards ceremony that doesn't resemble the Ringling Brothers auditions, or the Red Sox winning the World Series. *out-RAY* is in the outer limits of nincompoopray.

owlet, *n.* A who's who.

oxymoron (ahk-sih-MOR-ahn), *n.* A fracture of speech combining contradictory terms, as in "business ethics," "customer service," "driver education," "military intelligence," "vegetarian chili," "southwest culture," "rap music," "airport security," or "a fine madness." *AHK-suh-MOOR-ahn* is best at worst.

0

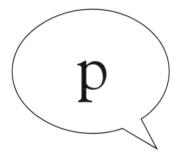

p

paean (PEE-un), *n.* Latin for "hymn to Apollo." A word homonymous with "peon" and "paeon." A paean is generally a song of joy or thanksgiving to celebrate the fact that, for instance, the baseball season ended *before* Thanksgiving; that someone discovered a vaccine against multi-level marketing; that the ugly rumor that Ozzy Osbourne was going straight was false; or that they finally solved the three-dimensional mathematics conundrum (whew!). *PEE-on* is acceptable only to *PEE-ons*.

pajamas (puh-JAH-muhz), *n.*, *pl.* In the '70s and '80s, the only safe things to sleep with. A restrictive slumber garment. *puh-JAM-uhz* is a favorite of Santa Monicrats and Hamptonians, and *JAM-eez* has a certain vogue among kindergarteners and sexually active geriatrics. *JAMA* could not be reached for comment.

palm (PAHM), *n.* Tall, thin tropical trees whose broad, leafy tops resemble the open human hand with nothing up its sleeve, uncharacteristically. *v.t.* To conceal something in the hand; to illegally dribble a basketball, when the game had rules.

paper shredder, *n.* A device designed to improve the output of creative writing classes, screenplay seminars, or publications for the financiallorn.

parvenu (PAHR-vuh-noo), *n.* An upstart, Johnny-come-tardily, nouveau Richeardo, etc. In West Palm, Marin, Greenwich, Bloomfield Hills, or Brentwood, one distinguished by the tow bar affixed to his chauffeurless (gasp!) Rolls; in Vermont or the English Midlands, a squatter (a resident for less than three hundred years). Mispronunciation is generally accentual, but may also appear as *par-VEN-yooh* or *PAR-venue* (a golf course).

patently (PAH-t'nt-lee), *adj.* Obviously, evidently, etc. Often used in a political sense, as in "If it looks like a duck, walks like a duck, and talks like a duck, it's patently a Quayle." *PAT-t'nt-lee* is acceptable only by Ms. Ethlie Ann Vare, coauthor of *Patently Female*, a work about lady inventors.

pathos (PAY-thos), *n.* A condition evoking sympathy, compassion, or pity, e.g. for one growing old in an express checkout lane; for one having to drive through a retirement area; for one not having a *Survivor*, *Growing Up Gotti*, or *Weakest Link* block on the telly; etc. *PATH-ose*, goodbye!

patina (puh-TEE-nuh), *n.* Non-ferrous rust; any microscopically thin coating, such as the "veneer of respectability" coating a horny priest or your garden-variety televangelist. "Dust" is God's protective

p

coating for furniture, which ladies insist upon wrenching from innocent surfaces every three days or so (gentlemen, correctly, once or twice a year). Corporate and/or political patina falls under the heading of "varnish." *PAT'n-uh* is more popular than correct.

peace (PEESS), *n.* 1. A tactical blunder. 2. In industrialized societies, the condition of temporary sanity. 3. In North America, a trough in hostilities allowing a fifth of the male population of Canada to flow south.

p

peccary (PEH-kuh-re), *n.* A not-quite-a-pig. An animal caught between a hock and a lard place. In the southwest U.S. it is known as "Javelina" (*hav-uh-LEE-nuh*), or wild boar, a close relative of *hav-uh-NUTHA,* or the domestic bore. *puh-KAIR-ee* is hairy.

pectoral (PEK-tuh-ruhl), *adj.* Of or about the chest muscle or heart area, where, on occasion, D cup runneth over.

Peking / Beijing (bay-ZHING, -JING). The top of the Peking order of names for the second largest city in China, according to Peiping Tom whose Beijing duck is renowned in Brooklyn Heights and among the congregations of Cucamonga.

penal (PEE-n'l), *adj.* Of punishment, or institutions now prescriptive of "rehabilitation" and other extracrookular activities.

penalize (PEE-n'l-eyes), *v.t.* To punish; to cause those with detention deficit disorder (DDD) to be held, against their will, in a structured environment offering full medical, dental, mortuarial, sexual, and narcotical benefits. (Who *wouldn't* be pissed!) *PEN-uh-lize* is unrehabilitative.

penile (PEE-nile), *adj.* Of or pertaining to the pee-pee. *PEEN'l* is a little short.

pensioner (PEN-shun-ur), *n.* One who looks forward to a five-day weekend, with two days off for *god* behavior. The pensioner is easily identified in late afternoon traffic by his distinctive automobile, which is equipped with the signature white Styrofoam cooler on the roof, right turn-signal flashing, and the gas cap door open.

p

Pepys (PEEPS), **Samuel** (1633–1703). Famous (among Japanese high-school students) English chronicler. A public servant, he had plenty of time during the workday to record rather vivid narratives of admiralty, court, and everyday life in his "diary," in which cipher was rifer. Name often pronounced otherwise by bloggers of the *PEP-si* generation.

peremptory (puh-REMP-tuh-re), *adj.* Imperious; dictatorial; judicially smug. As distinguished from, and commonly confused with, "pre-emptory," meaning having preference over others, as in buying or selling to the exclusion of others, as in the Martha Stewart School of stock liquidation.

persiflage (PUR-sih-flahzh), *n.* Flippancy. A conversational style representing the model to which the banal—i.e. those grounded in "you th' man," "do the math," "no problem," etc.—aspire, but who are commonly thwarted by the ass gene (with all apologies to the burro).

persona non grata (pur-SO-nuh nahn GRAH-tuh), *phr.* A person personally not acceptable, or, for instance, about as welcome as a grammarian at a rap session, an animal-rights activist at a biker bar, a speech pathologist at a Dixiecrat mixer, or a feminist at a Klan rally.

petulance (PEH-chuh-lunts), *adj*. Shortness of temper, patience, tipping, etc. Stock in t(i)rade of the longevitous, the fractious, and the Park Avenueish.

phenomenon (fih-NAH-muh-nahn), *n.* A word stricken from the "with-it" vocabulary. "Phenomena," like "species," is now both singular and plural. A phenome*NAHN*, now, is something seen but never explained, such as the sun, or seen but impossible to believe, such as the winner of a horse race or prize fight. As distinguished from "noumenon" (*NOO-muh-nahn*), which is something talked about but never seen, such as fiscal integrity or the sun in Detroit.

Philistine (FIH-luh-steen), *n.* According to the Bible, a member of a tribe of people credited with the invention of men's sleeveless shirts, women's prize fighting, Farelly brothers movies, reality TV, bachelor/bachelorette parties, competitive eating, art as

investment, goatees, groupies, wanna-bes, Hamptonians, right-wingers, leftovers, light beer, heavy
metal, subwoofers, monster trucks, smackdowns,
biker bars, Raiders fans, chauvinism, gay bashing,
Growing Up Gotti, and chewing gum. (Samson, the
fabled Israelite, is said to have regularly engaged
Philistines in mortal combat, wielding merely the
jawbone of a talk-show caller.) *fuh-LISS-tun* and *FIL-
us-tine* are equally optional. *FIL-o'-stahn* is acceptable
only if your refrigerator resides on your front porch.

phrenology (free-NAHL-uh-gee), *n.* From the classical Greek "phrenos," meaning "head up ass," the
ancients having put forth the quite easily believed
theory that the human brain is located closer to the
stomach than the cranium ("I have a gut feeling";
"My gut reaction was . . . ," etc.). Phrenology, then, is
the study of the shape and contour of the human
skull, in order to determine character, intent, fitness
for parole, etc., and is related to "physiognomy," or
the study of revealing or suspicious *facial* features,
seminars on which are regularly conducted at major
post offices, and which may also take into consideration the "most-wanted poster" section.

pianist (pe-ANN-ist), *n*. One who plays the piano-forte (*pe-ANN-uh-fort*), as opposed to one who plays *at* the pianoforte, or *PEE-un-ist*, variably mispronounced depending on how obscene the for(t)eplay.

Picabo (PIK-uh-bo, PEEK-uh-bo). As in Picabo Street, skier and victim of parental misnomicality. The only way to force *PEEK-uh-boo* out of Picabo is to add an "e" at the end, as in "canoe," or, horrors, another "o." Other than that, the slippery slope ends at *PEEK-uh-bo*.

picture (PIK-chur), *n*. In the litigious USA, an exhibit worth ten thousand pages minimum of trial transcript. In the event of an *adequate* defense, the parish will provide the frame. Note, if the picture is "fuzzy," it is usually of an UFO. If the modern canvas is blank or reeking of urine, soak the suckers another $10,000. *PIK-shur* is the feminine, *PIT-chur* the asinine.

pineal (PIE-nee-ul), *adj*. From the Latin "pinea," or "pine cone." Of a small, cone-shaped gland in the brain having no known function but materially influencing the shape of its immediate surroundings in the highest vertebrates. *PIN-nee-ul* is acceptable from eggheads and some pinheads.

piquant (PEE-kunt), *adj*. Pleasantly pungent or slightly smoldering, from where is got "medium picante" or other three-alarm sauces; also, stimulating to the senses, even when sauced. Lexicographically: sharp, biting, provocative, productive of royalties, etc. *PIH-kwunt* now, tends to make the smoke alarm yawn.

piranha (puh-RAH-nuh), *n*. A beast said to be able to strip the flesh from unwary prey in less than a New York critic minute. *puh-RAHN-yuh* is not quite as toothsome.

pis aller (pee zah-LAY), *n*. French for the "last resource," or, popularly, the last resort, where, backed against the wall, the human being may even be forced to employ such unthinkables as thinking, or (horrors) reflection, before getting peed on.

plastic surgeon, *n*. A cos*med*ic, who will stretch out the payments for you.

plethora (PLEH-thuh-ruh), *n*. Popularly (but erroneously), abundance. Originally, superabundance, distention, swelling, etc. A word commonly (over)used by pathological orators. *pleh-THOR-uh* is incorrect.

poesy (POE-uh-zee), *n*. The ancient (your father's aunt's tutor's drug dealer's) reference to poetry. *POE-zy*, no-zy!

> *The art of poesy*
> *Was formerly roesy,*
> *Its songs of metered line;*
> *Alas, that craft*
> *Now lies scuttled by the daft*
> *In unconscious streams of proesy.*

poet, *n*. A scribe having taken a turn for the verse.

poinsettia (poyn-SET-te-uh), *n*. After J. R. Poinsett (circa 1779–1851), American ambassador to Mexico, 1825–29, Secretary of War (now "Defense," in order to accommodate the euphemistically lusty), 1837–41. The poinsettia is a tropical shrub with red "petals," used as a potted plant to delight potted revelers during the Twelve Months of Christmas. *poyn-SET-uh* is the common infraction.

pointillist (PWAHN-t'l-ist), *n.* A technician who prepares tests for color-blindness. If you are not color-blind, you will see an outline of Pissaro's beard. *POIN-tuh-list* ain't half bad.

politically incorrect, *phr.* "Impolitic," for the windy.

porcine (PAWR-sign), *adj.* Of or like swine, a species featuring the Chauvinist pig, the Howie Long, and other prime cuts of butt.

porcupine (PAWR-cue-pine), *n.* "Spinous hog," with a license to quill, especially those, we can only hope, who pronounce it as *PORKY-pine*.

posthumous (PAHS-chuh-mus), *adj.* Arising after assassination, murder, execution, ambush, whacking, etc. *PAHS-tyoo-mus*, non.

postlude, *n.* The underture.

potable (POE-tuh-b'l), *adj.* Suitable for drinking; as in water made suitable for drinking by the addition of whiskey. *PAHT-uh-b'l* by the potty crowd and other Jeopardy losers.

potato (puh-TAY-toe), *n.* A plant of the nightshade family, its root falling on hard times as "French fries." Potatoes come in two sizes: small and Philip Morris RNC contributions. Proper renderings of the vegetable are as follows: parslied new, hashed with onions, baked, mashed with garlic in a heavy cream, latke(ed), or escalloped with garlic, heavy cream, and Swiss or parmesan cheese. *puh-TAH-toe,* in the shower.

prehensile (pre-HEN-s'l), *adj.* From the Latin "prehensus," meaning "to seize." Said of an anatomical feature of creatures of the simian persuasion who hang around in the jungle and, from the evidence, WWF events, Pay-Per-Viewings, White Sox home games, and tanning parlors. A low forehead, prognathous jaw and a rather strained relationship with personal hygiene are also common. *pre-HEN-sile* tells a tail, also.

P

prelude (PREL-yood), *n*. As with a wildfire, an Oscar speech, or a car chase through Los Angeles, a prelude (overture) is more easily started than stopped. Just ask Franz Liszt, if you can find him. (And if Liszt wants to say *pray-LUID*, who are we to argue!)

prenuptial (pre-NUP-shul), *adj*. Pertaining to an agreement banking on divorce. A matrimonial 401(k). *pre-NUPT-shul* has irreconcilable differences.

presage (PREH-sij), *n*. An ominous forewarning, such as "Mission accomplished!" "Bring 'em on!" "Let the good times roll in Iraq . . . ," etc. *prih-SAYJ* is equally sage.

presidents (PREH-zuh-dunts), *n*. Intercontinental scarecrows; usurpers of bureaucratic privilege; pawns of the high-fructose corn syrup lobby. *PREZ-dints* seems to be capital, Capitolly.

prestigious (press-TIJ-us), *adj*. Then (sixteenth century): deceitful or dishonorable; marked by conniving or trickery. Now: honorable or highly thought of; marked by beachfront property in Connecticut, or "Doctors, Lawyers, and Indian chiefs."

That is, doctors with fewer than seven convictions for prescription fraud; lawyers not having been disbarred over nondisclosure of Mob collusion; and Indian chiefs having survived the pogroms of the usurpers of beachfront property in Connecticut. Other of the "prestigious" include clergy not on the sex-offender hotline; psychologists with postgraduate degrees and who are endorsed by Jerry Springer; "A" list actors; major leaguers who miraculously score negative on the urinalysis; and former hostages of space aliens.

preventive (prih-VEN-tiv), *adj*. Protectic; prophylactic. *n*. Something that protects or prophylacticates, such as a condom, i.e., a galosh worn during inclement weather indoors. *prih-VEN-tuh-tiv* is marginally unacceptable argumentatively, except around the condominia.

primer (PRIM-ur), *n*. A small book on (academic) fundamentals, typically used as wallpaper on subbasements of the underfunded and dilapidated American school system. Students are left to subsist on teachers. A *PRY-mur* is the part of a cartridge that explodes the bullet toward Fundamentalists.

primum mobile (PRY-mum MO-buh-lee), *n*. In ancient astronomy, the silly theory that the outermost ring of ten celestial rings is the prime mover of the others, causing the planets and stars to move around Earth, when everyone *knows* that all heavenly bodies revolve around a ring with a 3-karat solitaire.

princess (PRIN-sus), *n*. See "pumpkin."

prius (PRI-us), *n*. Greek for "first." Name of a model of a Toyota automobile powered by a hybrid engine achieving 25,000 mpg, or some such. Detroit could not be reached for comment. *PRE-us* is not quite as roadworthy.

proboscis (pruh-BAH-sus), *n*. A nose, especially a funny-looking one. The search engine or sighting device used by the aristocrat to *look* down, in surveillance of the sucker, the sinner, or the sot. In the lower orders it is said to merely smell up the place, on its way to a "job."

promenade (prah-muh-NADE), *n*. An avenue, a deck, or a hall, for strutting your stuff. *v.t.* To strut your stuff, if your strut is not too stuffed to strut. *prah-muh-NAHD* and the notorious *lem-uh-NAHD* are second bananas but go well with stuffed shirts strutting their stuff.

pronunciation (pruh-nun-see-A-shun), *n.* It is easy to mispronounce this word as *pro-noun-se-A-shun* (a marathon of pronouns?), as did most of the participants (and judges) in the seventy-fifth annual National Spelling Bee.

prostate (PRAHS-tate), *n.* A male gland surrounding the urethra, which assists in the flow of sperm and which, in certain chatty rooms, stands accused of contributing to heir pollution. Very frequently mispronounced as *PRAHS-trate*, mostly by those claiming membership in the Misfortune 500, snuff dippers, tailgaters, Junior Leaguers, barflies, motorsportsmen quoted as saying "I ain't never paid for it and I don't need no damn Viagra!," and men over the age of fifty with more than three tank-top shirts in their formal wardrobes. Carcinomic surgery side effects include impotence and inconsequence—in the morning you awake stiff in all the wrong places.

p

protein (PRO-tee-un), *n*. The amino-peptide contributing to the A—bra size of female—and the DDD bra size of male—bodybuilders. *PRO-teen*, averagely.

psychiatrist (suh-KIGH-uh-tryst) *n*. A physician who seldom physishes; a clinician trained in the fine tuning of primal urges, charging substantially more than a psychologist but less than a plumber. Typically treats depression and suicidal tendencies of undercover "non-smoking area" informers; over-medicates colleagues suffering from postpartum anxiety from the loss of patients having received "Five Sample Viagra Pills Shipped in a Discreet Wrapper"; ministers to the uncontrollable guffawing of phony bankruptcy declarants; proposes management therapy for the suppressed joy of hit-and-runners in the Winn-Dixie parking lot; and allays the fleeting guilt of Canadians associated with cheap tipping, among other things. *sigh-KIGH-ih-tryst* needs help.

pterodactyl (ter-uh-DAK-t'l), *n*. An enormous flying dinosaur similar to a B-52. Its extinction is hailed daily by commuters with windshields having been carpet-bombed by pigeons. *TER-uh-dak-t'l* is just terrible.

puissant (PWIH-s'nt, PYOO-uh-s'nt), *adj.* Mighty; omnipotent; immortal. Used mainly in an heroic sense to describe such egomaniacs as Alexander, Napoleon, Rush Limbaugh, etc. *PWIS-n't* is airroneous.

Pulitzer (PULL-it-ser), *n.* After Joseph Pulitzer (1847–1911), of "Prize" fame. Newspaper publisher Pulitzer became widely known for his papers' aggressive competition against "Hearst Journalism," an oxymoron of the time (1880s). Pulitzer Prizes are awarded annually for various categories of writing. *PYOO-lit-zer* is incorrect, while *POOH-lit-ser* seems to be popular among nonwinners.

puma (PYOO-muh), *n.* Mountain lion, cougar; close-to-extinct denizen of southwest USA, which is also home to the endangered bobcat and missing lynx. *POO-muh* being alive and swell.

pumpkin (PUMP-kin), *n.* A gourd which, when hollowed out, contains about as much horse sense as a human bean. *PUNG-kin* is used by doting male parents and grandparents to address allegedly virginal daughters and/or granddaughters. Synonym: "princess."

pun, *n.* Wit decaffeinated and served at room temperature.

purloin (pur-LOIN), *v.* For celebrity has-beens: To furtively or surreptitiously steal, in the manner of a shoplifter, so that no one will catch on, except surveillance cameras, paparazzi, *Daily Variety*, and CNN, giving kleptomania a bad name. Files, documents, and exhibits regularly purloined from the National Archives, NSA, and CIA by ex–White House staff, foreign diplomats, and street people from Avenue D fall under the headings of "statistical error," "inventory shrinkage," or "clipboard malfunction." *PURloin*, for boosters.

pustule (PUHS-chool), *n.* A container of pus. Containers (sacs, blisters, pimples, craniums) vary in size and volume and are detectable by discoloration or, in the event of insurance, by palpation of the pocketbook. *PUHS-tyool* is also cool.

qualm (KWAHM), *n*. Compunction; misgiving. Originally, qualm implied a feeling of nausea or severe uneasiness at wrongdoing, since eased by hegemony and organized religion. *KWAHLM*, in error.

quantity (KWAHN-tuh-tee), *n*. Commonly, an amount sufficient to atone for quality. *KWAHN-uh-tee* is current corn. Standard measure:

2 pints = 1 quart
4 quarts = 1 gallon
31.5 gallons = 1 barrel
2 barrels = 1 hogshead
100 hogsheads = 1 senate

quash / squash, *v.* Currently used interchangeably, mostly by cavalier editors and broadcasters. To quell, suppress, or put down, typically in a manner lacking ceremony. "Squash" is the coarser usage, in that it inevitably evokes horrific images of vital organic fluid(s) leaking from the carcass of a rapist, terrorist, pedophile, fraud-by-wire artist, computer hacker, recidivist, neo-Nazi, guy in the boom-box low-rider behind you, etc.

quasi (KWAY-zie, KWAH-zee), *adj., pref.* Now used mainly as a prefix to mean "in a sense but not entirely," as in "a Hammond is a quasi-organ;" "a keyboard is a quasi-piano" or "he was a quasi-sword-swallower, because he always stopped at the hilt."

Quebec (kwih-BEK), *n.* The part of Canada containing the seceding-in-any-given-year provincial

French, and which is known as the "Appalachia of the North." Pronounced as *kay-BEK* by Quebecois, indigenous hockeycasters, and Americans who usually find themselves in the penalty box *nuh-GOE-se-ate-ing* with *suh-NAHR-ee-o*.

queer (KWEER), *adj*. Other than ordinary, establishment, commonly understood, blindly accepted. Said of those who find, among other things, that sleeping with a Panang lawyer can be quite titillating indeed.

query (KWIHR-ee, KWEAR-ee), *v*. To question (a person); to interview with doubt, i.e. forensic or treasonous curiosity, as when Jane Fonda fell apart on *Larry King Live*.

quorum (KWAR-um), *n*. A word that starts off toward "quarrel" (*KWAR-ul*), takes a slight detour, but never loses its way. A quorum, of course, is the number of recalcitrants, stonewallers, and malcontents needed to dump on the rules committee and assail the compliance officer while revising *Robert's Rules of Disorder*. *KWOR-um* is also correct.

q

Rajasthan (RAH-juh-stahn), *n.* State of northwest central India. Capital: Jaipur (*JI-pour*). Bledfellows are Pakistan, Hindustan, Tajikistan, Kyrgystan, Dagestan, Khazikstan, Baluchistan, Afghanistan, Uzbekistan, Turkmenistan, and Laurelstan.

rap, *n.* Noise characterized by discourse rich in the absence of prepositions, articles, and adverbs. There are three kinds of rap: A-rap (the Will Smith variety); B-rap, which once *did* contain an adverb, thereby voiding the recording contract; and C-rap, or what we have today.

raspberry (RAZ-bair-ee, RAZ-bur-ee), *n*. The seed of a rhubarb, popular in Shea Stadium or Ebbets Field.

ratio (RAY-show), *n*. The centerpiece around which proportional mathematicians decorate tables of fractional incomprehensibility, causing overpopulation in Mass Communications and Physical Education curricula in the USA. *RAY-she-oh* is the product of the syllably challenged and indentured CPAs.

ratiocination (rah-she-o-s'n-AY-shun), *n*. Exact thinking; reasoning using formal logic. Hence, a train of thought whereby the caboose is liable to, at any moment, appear in front of the locomotive.

ration (RAH-shun), *n*. In wartime, one's fixed allotment (depending on one's access to the black market). *v.t.* To parcel out (keeping the greater portion, including bribes, for oneself). *RAY-shun* is also popular.

realtor (REE-ul-tur), *n.* A listing agent, usually to the right. The downgrade of a used-car salesman. Contracts/proposals make *War and Peace* look like an easy read. *REE-luh-tur* is the abiding pronunciation of new "owners" of leaky roofs and tipsy foundations. *REEL-tur* is fishy.

recluse (REH-kloos), *n.* One whose WELCOME mat faces out and lies directly in front of the moat. *WRECK-loose* is not far off the mark.

redress (rih-DRESS), *v.t.* To correct or amend, as in the first ten redressments to the Constitution of the United States, allowing such enlightened compensatories as the preservation and protection of the national prurience and the right of the people to bare their arms and peaceably dissemble. *REE-dress,* no.

reiterate (re-IH-tuh-rate), *v.t.* The "irregardless" of repetition, irrespective of iteration.

renege (rih-NIG), *v.* To fail to fulfill an obligation, promise, etc., hoping that none of the suckers remembers any of those pesky little planks in the platform. *re-NEG* and *rih-NEEG* are the renegades.

repast (rih-PAST), *n*. An annoyance interfering with man's natural appetite for Martinis. One main repast per day is about all a thinking drinker can stand. *REE-past* is not.

reproduction, *n*. "A fortuitous concourse" of Adams.

reptile (REP-tile, REP-t'l), *n*. Any of an order of Reps, public *serpents*, or primitive, leathery-skinned bushwhackers. "Reptilian" can be used either as a slur or a compliment, depending on which side of the aisle you prefer to slink, with all apologies to the snakes. Sci-Fi hacks are known to adorn their theses with reptile-like creatures, during their not-infrequent lapses of imagination. The plumber's snake is often found coiled tightly around your wallet.

requital (rih-QUITE-ul), *n*. Revenge; payback. The special and rather enduring quality separating man from the Higher Animals, and supplying middle Americans, saloon goons, and folk-hero groupies with two thirds of their conversation: "What goes around comes around, man." *REK-wit-ul* is best served cold.

respiratory (RES-pruh-tor-ee, rih-SPY-ruh-tor-ee), *adj.* Of the process by which a living organism takes a breath. The respiratory rate of Americans is controlled by Congress, members of which are able to take away the electorate's breath by arguing that their $23,000 cost-of-living "adjustment" is *not* a pay raise. *RES-puh-ruh-tor-ee* optionalizes.

respite (RES-put), *n.* A break or relief, especially from something disagreeable or laborious. For instance, after 1971 and the development of "wall of sound" technology, popular singers and entertainers were no longer required to have actual musical abilities. Whew! Today they can focus their energies on what really counts: wowing the audience with their wardrobes (or, in many cases, the lack thereof). *re-SPITE* ain't rite.

résumé (REH-zuh-may, reh-zuh-MAY), *n.* A summary, largely ungrammatical, of one's fitness for employment; next to the political platform and the personal ad, the most accepted form of lying. *RES-uh-may* is not employable.

Riefenstahl (REE-fun-stahl), **Leni** (LAY-nee) (1902–2003). German cinematographer. Produced 1934 Nazi party flick entitled *Triumph of the Wardrobe* in an attempt to upstage future Super Bowl halftime pageantry. Home team lost.

rodeo (ro-DAY-o, RO-de-o), *n.* If *ro-DAY-o*, a zone known for the becoiffery, bejewelery, and bedrapery of the molls of CFOs, PolitiCEOs, and other well-heeled riff-raff, or a ballet by Copland. If *RO-de-o*, a competition among cowboys for the consumption of liniment (mostly externally). The first cowboy competition is said to have occurred in Prescott (*PRES-kut*), Arizona, on July 4, 1888. The cowboy competition that took place in the streets of Tombstone, Arizona, in 1881, however, was much more entertaining, with daily re-enactments taking place today in most major metropolitan areas of the USA.

Roget (ro-ZHAY), **Peter Mark** (1779–1869). Famous English physician and lexicographer, whose name is synonymous. Roget's Thesaurus dwarfs all other works of its kind, and is known in some circles as TyrannoThesaurus Rex. *ro-GAY,* no way.

romance (ro-MANTS), *adj.* Of a language or having to do with any of several languages derived from Low Latin: Spanish, Italian, Portuguese, etc. *n.* A type of literature (*RO-mants*) or relationship characterized by much imagination, in the highest forms of which male protagonists are said to even remove their socks before sex.

roof (ROOHF), *n.* A temporary covering for a house—attached by staples after one has paid for a screwing. *ROOF* or *RUUF* is the sound made by the creature in actual control of the house.

Roosevelt (RO-zuh-velt). Specifically Franklin Delano. Next to JFK and Harry Truman, the most oft-quoted Democratic American president—by Republicans. The oft-quoting is mainly off-quoting, by both Republicans *and* Democrats, particularly when it comes to the Pearl Harbor address. ". . . a date that will live in infamy . . ." does indeed live in infamy as ". . . a *day* that will live in infamy. . . ." *ROO-zuh-velt* rues.

rotunda (ro-TUN-duh), *n*. A building designed in the shape of a U.S. citizen but having the edge in weight, slightly. *RAHT'n-duh* is less shapely.

route (ROOHT), *n*. A line of travel leading *out* of Detroit, Newark, East St. Louis, Compton, Scottsdale, Miami, Baghdad, etc. Conventionalized as *ROUT*, especially by anyone having been detoured through, stuck in, or tripticked near any of those cities.

row, *n*., *v*. There are two known pronunciations for this word and three unknown. Having won the coin toss, the author has elected to deal with the former. You can't row (*RO*) your boat in a row house, oar so it seems, but you can have a row (*RAU*), and probably will, in a row house. A "rowan" (*RAU-un*), now, is another name for an ash tree, with Carl Rowan (*RO-un*), a solid-as-oak commentator, objecting.

Rowling (RO-ling), **J. K.** British author whose book sales are said to eclipse even those of certain alternative lexicographers, and who is rumored to have proposed changing the name of Washington, D.C., to the Republic of Hogwords. *RAU-ling*, in Whitechapel or Fort Smith.

rule of thumb, *phr.* In North America, an axiom having given way to the Rule of "Finger," closely attended by the Rule of Mob.

ruse (ROOZ), *n.* A deception of more ingenuity than a trick but less than an artifice; used once in a *wile* by women. *ROOSS* is also useable.

r

Salisbury (SOLZ-ber-e), *n.* The county seat of Wilt-shire, England, and the site of Stonehenge; also, the butt of hamburger jokes, after Dr. J. H. Salisbury, early twentieth-century London physician who had a *steak* in the minced-beef game.

salmon (SAM-un), *n.* An upscale fish and down-market literary metaphor. *SAWL-mun* and *SELL-mun* are alive and well, mon!

Salome (suh-LOW-mee, SAL-uh-may), *n.* In the Bible, an aristocratic floozy who turned out to be her mother's daughter, and who, to get ahead in the game, choreographed the death of John the Baptist.

S&M, *abbr.* Stock Market.

sangfroid (SAHN-FRWAH), *n.* French for "cold blood." Popularly: grace under pressure; coolness under fire; composure under interview; equanimity under Bush. A fantasy that came in with Hemingway and went out with Nixon.

sanguine (SANG-wuhn), *adj.* Optimistic, blood-thirsty, red-blooded (on the outside), cheerful, murderous. A decidedly undecided word virtually unable to make up its mind, whose Latin root, *Sanguineus*, means "woman in shoe store."

sardonyx (sahr-DAH-niks), *n.* The birthstone of wit.

satrap (SAY-trap), *n.* A petty tyrant, as undistinguished from your boss. *SAY-trump* and you're fired.

satyr (SAY-tur), *n.* In Greek mythology, a deity who *fauned* on Bacchus. Popularly, a male nymphomaniac, usually pictured with the body of a man, the liver of a sot, and the head of a lounge lizard. In other words, something out of *SAT-ur-day* night fever. *SAH-tur*, optionally.

Saudi (SAW-dee, sah-OOH-dee), *n.* Saudi Arabia; a Saudi Arabian. *SAW-dee* is the predominant pronunciation of the West and those who do not luxuriate in the clerical oil of atavism.

sauté (saw-TAY, so-TAY), *v.t.* From the French "sauter," meaning "to leap." To cook over a fire hastily in fat or oil, or, politically, to leap at a news conference in order to pull your fat *out* of the fire. Four-star chefs seem to be satisfied with *saw-TAY*, while the heavyweights and Canadians stand fast with *salt-AY*.

savoir faire (sav-wahr FAR), *n.* French for "Don't invite the Marx Brothers again," meaning tact, propriety, knowing precisely what to do—or not do—in any given situation. In other words, you wouldn't

S

intentionally pass gas at an afternoon tea thrown by Martha Stewart. You wouldn't deliberately park a van marked CENTER FOR DISEASE CONTROL in front of an All You Can Eat restaurant. However, you *would* invite al Zarkawe to a wine and anthrax tasting, and you *would* hold your lunch down until you've exited the presidential press conference, or at least you'd try to.

scenario (suh-NAIR-e-o), *n*. Formerly of six syllables, this word has been abused so often by vitamin-enriched newscasters and canonized commentators that it is currently down to four. It's an arrangement of scenes in a motion picture, play, soap opera, etc., that you wish to be a part of instead of moldering as a field correspondent, novelist, hooker, bartender, waitress, cubiclist, or pop psychologist. *suh-NAHR-e-o*, for the lingua-funkists.

schizophrenia (skit-suh-FREE-nee-uh), *n*. A delusional dysfunction characterized by paranoia, incoherence, and "multiple personalities." Occasionally referred to as "U.S. foreign policy." *skit-suh-FREN-ee-uh* is suspiciously more popular.

schlemiel (shluh-MEEL), *n.* The chumpion. One who, when walking, leaves a trail of slime.

schlimazel / shlimazel (shlih-MAY-z'l), *n.* The chumpee. One, typically, with bug splatter on the *inside* of the windshield.

scimitar (SIM-uh-t'r), n. A long curved sword, traditionally worn around the neck of "infidels." *SIM-ih-tar* ain't as sharp.

scion (SIGH-un), *n.* An SOB (Son Of a Bigwig) or DOG (Daughter Of the Gentry). Birthrights include *your* former 401(k) and the benighted generosity of zombified stockholders. Generally a scion is a descendant, but the term is often used by homicide investigators and tabloid reporters in reference to an ascendant descendant. *SKIGH-ahn* is sigh-worthy.

Scotchman (SKAHTCH-mun), *n.* One with a different speech impediment than an Irishman, a Welshman, or the governor of California.

S

scourge (SKURJ), *n*. An affliction, severe punishment, or misery, such as a plague, famine, ecological disaster, Renaissance festival, etc. Also, a device or instrument for the *inflicting* of misery, such as a whip, cat-o-nine-tails, granola bar, microphone, Palahniuk novel, etc. *SKORJ* is okay during prime time.

secession (sih-SESH-un), *n*. Formal withdrawal, in writing, inked in blood. Before the commencement of the U.S. (un)Civil War, seven southern states withdrew from the union: South Carolina, Mississippi, Alabama (who would miss them?), Florida, Georgia, Louisiana, and Texas; these were followed after the actual beginning of the war by Virginia, Arkansas, North Carolina, and Tennessee. The North "won." *see-SESH-un* does not succeed.

second opinion (uh-PIN-yun), *med. Phr*. A notion thought to be less incorrect than the first.

seer (SE-ur), *n*. An East Indian unit of weight equal to 1/100 of a clairvoyant, remote viewer, sensitivitist, palmist, new-ager, negative ionizer, psychic friend, tarotian, toenail reader, or anyone who tests positive for $9/gallon Scotch. *SEER*, or *SEAR*, is queer.

segue (SAY-gway), v. From the Italian "seguire," meaning "to follow." In music: to continue without a break into the next passage, forcing half of the percussionists into the men's room to bum a joint off of the principal bassist. Popularly, to slide from one embarrassment into another press leak. *SEH-gway* is good enough if you're bidding on one (a Segway vehicle) or if you're one of the few to have ever fallen off of one.

semi (SEH-me, SEH-my). Prefix meaning half, almost, not quite, etc., as in Wolf Blitzer's or Chuck Norris's "beard" (are they beards or just five-o'clock shadows?) or the signature facial sprouts ("goatees") of the Tufted generation. The expression "semi" (*SEM-I*) by itself refers to a semitrailer, or "big rig" in truckstopese. A Seminole (*SEM-uh-nole*), by the way, is not half of an Indian.

serpentine (SUR-pun-teen, SUR-pun-tine), *adj.* In or of the shape, form, style, manner, etc., of a serpent or snake, the oil of which beast is said to light the lamps of the Faithful and serve as the principal illumination of Middle Earth.

shamrock (SHAM-rahk), *n*. Cubic zirconia.

sheik / sheikh, *n*. A title of respect accorded an Arab or Moslem executive type. Currently, *SHAKE* is chic and *SHEEK* is jake.

sherbet (SHUR-but), *n*. To accommodate their moronic contemporaries, modern lexicon-artists and metathetic apologists acknowledge *SHUR-burt* as a legitimate alternative. They also list the absence of apostrophes in commercial signage under the heading of "cute."

short-lived (SHORT-LYVD, SHORT-LIVD), *adj*. Mercifully timed. Timing is everything. According to the late but renowned practitioner I. M. Elmer, Ph.D., time is relative and goes slowest when you're having elective dental surgery and fastest when you're having sex in a moving elevator. *SHORT-LYVD* is correcter in that it speaks to life, not living.

sieve (SIHV), *n*. The device used by the Border Patrol, the INS, and port authorities to snare terrorists. Luckily, since September 11, 2001, the arrests of little old ladies in wheelchairs without CCW (Concealed Cuticle Weaponry) permits by crack units of federal airport inspectors have increased exponentially. (It is a shame, however, that all bureaucrats get blamed for the bungling of just a few thousand.)

silicon (SIL-ih-kun), *n*. A nonmetallic element used in the manufacture of semiconductors. Often confused with "silicone" (*SIL-uh-kone*), a compound of silicon used in the manufacture of sexiconductors.

slovenly (SLUH-vun-lee), *adj*. Appearing never to have had a close brush with soap; able to stave off seemliness with the best of them. Frequently said of those prone to questions such as "Is there life after Megadeth?" or "Shall the Mick inherit the earth?" etc. *SLOW-vun-lee* is down and dirty.

snob (SNAHB), *n*. Formerly, a crude lowlife or wretch. Currently, a wretch unrepentant for possessing good taste.

solace (SAH-lus), *n*. A condition about as rare today as a two-parent TV sitcom, a federal budget proposal weighing less than a tractor, a svelte suburbanite, or a maternity shop at a retirement resort. *SO-lus* is less consoling.

sommelier (suh-mull-YAY), *n.* Originally an eighteenth-century French court official in charge of pack animals and beasts of burden, intractable creatures having since received the charity of a taxonomic upgrade to "waitstaff." Currently, a wine steward or stewardess. *suh-MAWL-ee-ay* or *suh-MAWL-yay* usually squeak by.

S

species (SPEE-sheez), *n.* A kind or type. A subclass of a genus. For example, man (species) is a Homo (genus) sapien (wise, discerning, etc., despite the persistence of evidentiary challenges). *SPEE-seez*, no.

statistics (stuh-TIS-tiks), *n.* The art of brandishing facts and/or figures for use in the several artful pursuits. Certain facts and figures are solid and predictable, such as: a) Annual highway deaths in America: 45,000+. b) Annual homicides in America: 23,000+. c) Annual 911 calls from the Detroit Tigers' bullpen: 162. *stuh-STIS-tiks* is the usual catcher.

status (STAY-tus), *n.* Rank; position; standing. A state of affairs or, among the social set, the state of stares while putting on airs. *STAT-us* is less elite.

Steinway yellowfin, *n.* A piano tuna.

Stephen / Steven (STEF-un / STEVE-un, STEE-fun), *pn.* *Male* given names, at this writing. "Stephen" should never be pronounced as *STEVE-un*, no matter how many macabre bestsellers you churn out.

strength (STRENGTH), *n.* A human condition requiring the presence of muscles. In the USA the popularity of muscles is such that the expression "on the muscle" is heard even more often than old standards such as "season's greedings," "please pass the crack pipe," "hit and run," and "what th' hell happened to my pension?" (Those with thin skin usually show their muscles the most.) *STRENTH* is rather anemic.

Styrofoam (STY-ruh-foam), *n.* A packing material lighter, but more flavorful, than rice cakes. *STY-ro-foam* is acceptable from those who can't tell the difference and from card-carrying members of the wine-in-a-box crowd, without being piggish on the subject.

submariner (sub-muh-REE-nur), *n*. This word is usually pronounced as *sub-MAIR-uh-nur* by civilians and naval desk jockeys but surfaces as *sub-muh-REE-nur* among the boys in the boats. Tom Brokaw's *The Greatest Generation* was pretty much "rigged for silent running" on the subject.

subsidiary (sub-SID-ee-air-ee), *n*. One controlled by another (very common in a socialist democracy). *sub-SID-uh-rare-ee* and *sub-SID-uh-ree* are the faults.

succinct (suck-SINKT), *adj*. Concise, clear, brief. The enemy of modern journalism or oratory. *suh-SINKT* sucks.

Sunni (SOO-nee), *n*. Traditionalist sect of Islam, Shiites (*SHE-ites*) being the sectual deviates. *SUN-ee* works as well.

superannuate (soo-pur-ANN-yuh-wait), *v.t.* To pension off, buy out, etc., in order to replace someone with a younger, cheaper embezzler.

superfluous (soo-PURR-floo-us), *adj.* Plethorafluous; redundant; too much, already! . . . as in "(super)star," "(super)model," or page numbers in a dictionary. The abundant mispronunciation is *soo-PURR-ful-us*.

supine (soo-PINE), *adj.* Lying on the back, face-up—expectant of a missionary. *SOO-pine* is divine, Sister!

sycophant (SIH-kuh-funt), *n.* A climber; a lowlife flatterer of the powerful, the heroic, or the influential, currently without prospect in pol-light society. *PSYCHO-funt* is incorrect but evocative.

syllogism (SIH-luh-jih-zum), *n.* A form of logic where common sense is given notice to vacate the premises.

synecdoche (suh-NEK-duh-ke), *n.* This household word refers to a figure of speech wherein the specific becomes the general. For example, "our daily bread" means food in general and the expression "The pen is mightier than the sword" means that writers are more powerful than critics. Mispronunciation ranges from *SIN-uh-doke* to *SIN-ek-doosh* from Baja to Schenectady.

S

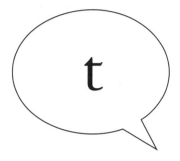

tabloid (TAH-bloyd), *n.* A newsance. The bible according to Queen James. Mispronunciation ranges anywhere from *JUR-nul* and *DAY-lee* to *peer-e-AHD-uh-kul.*

Tao (DOW, DAU), *n.* The guiding principle of Taoism, which was founded by Lao-tzu in the sixth century B.C. The Tao is taken to be the natural process by which all things change. The principle must be strictly adhered to in order to achieve a life of complete harmony, which, in turn, will enable postulants to achieve oneness with the universe, realize unimagined prosperity (if the DOW is up), and hit all the green lights on the way to the mall.

tarpaulin (TAHR-puh-lun, TAHR-paw-lun), *n.* Tar-impregnated canvas. Its most prominent use, aside from Boy Scout housing, was in the protecting of infield grass prior to the ballpark pogroms and the desecration of Wrigley Field in the late twentieth century. *tahr-PO-le-in* being all too common.

Tarzan (TAHR-zun, TAHR-zan), *pn.* An English gentleman (Lord Greystoke) forced to live in a wretched jungle but who, totally repelled by the fog, the pageantry, the warm beer, and the lack of First- and Second-Amendment rights, was eventually repatriated to Africa.

teat (TEET), *n.* The protuberance on a (preferably female) breast, through which milk may or may not pass in the suckling of young (ages one day through fifty-nine years). Over the age of fifty-nine it is considered a fixation. *TIT* ain't it, but *t'EAT* has possibilities.

theater (THEE-uh-tur), *n.* A place where large doses of popcorn, Coca-Colas, and chocolate bars serve to anesthetize the senses against histrionics, theatrics, foul language, disturbing performances, and other antics of the audience. *thee-A-tur*, then, is okay under the *circustances*, or anywhere in Kentucky.

Theresa / Teresa (tuh-REE-suh, tuh-REE-zuh), *pn.* It's only *tuh-RAY-zuh* in Heinz' sight.

thingamabob (THING-uh-muh-bahb), *n.* A thinga-majig; hence, a contraption, curwhibble, foppet, trumperyte, Rube Goldberger, etc.

Thoreau (thuh-ROE), **Henry** (1817–1862). Poet; journalist; pencil-maker; paranaturalist; jailbird. Ate potatoes; sauntered; played solitaire; wrote English sentences; preferred beachfront real estate. Born old; died young. Correct pronunciation is *HEN-re*, with love.

threshold (THRESH-hold), *n.* An exit through which one has mistakenly entered. In psychology, the point at which a patient's pocket is no longer pickable and a cure is thus effected. *THREH-shold*, where anything goes.

tiara (te-AIR-uh, te-AHR-uh), *n.* A woman's bejeweled or decorative headdress; the Pope's triple crown. (Who knew he kept race horses!) Originally, an ancient Persian headdress. (Ancient Persia, today, is known as Ancient Iran.)

Tijuana (tee-uh-WAH-nuh, tee-WAH-nuh), *n.* The utter side of San Diego. Home of miracle cures, affordable Viagra, Ugly Americans in bars and behind bars, and, thank the Gods, accordion players on DVD. *TEE-uh-WAHN-uh*, duh.

timorous (TIH-muh-rus), *adj.* Hesitant; fearfully expectant, like a rat before a snake or a lounge lizard before a feminist. *TIME-ur-us* does time.

titular (TIH-chuh-lur), *adj.* Of one who heads an office, without responsibility of duty, or one, in an office of responsibility, without a head—as in the Director of the CIA, NSA, NSC, INS, FAA, FBI, DEA, ATF, Secret Service, Border Patrol, Agricultural

Service, NORAD, etc. *TIT-yoo-lur* and *TIT-chuh-lur* are common protuberances.

Tolkien (TOEL-keen), **John Ronald Reuel** (1892–1973). Author of popular pentology ("trilogy" for outsiders), *Lord of the Rings*, a Hobbit-forming novel written in order to make Ents meet and with an Eye on immortality. *TOEL-kin* is acceptable from trilologists.

tomato (tuh-MAY-toe), *n.* You say *tuh-MAY-toe*, Julia Child says *tuh-MAH-toe*; you say *puh-TAY-toe*, Bart Simpson says *spud-TAH-toe*. *tuh-MAY-toe, spud-TAH-toe*, let's call the whole thing. . . . In restaurants, a waste product, except for the core and ends which are served sliced upon request.

toreador (TAWR-ee-uh-dawr), *n.* A bullfighter on horseback. (The horse's term for it was "estupido.") "Matador" is correct for a bullfighter on foot, or under foot, as the case may be. *tawr-AY-uh-dor* is incorrect (Bizet was, after all, French).

Tortilla Flat (toar-TEE-uh FLAT). This place-name, in Arizona, east of Phoenix, is invariably pronounced

t

(and written) as Tortilla Flats. Out-of-state media personnel, however, usually get it right.

toucan (TOO-kan, TOO-kahn), *n.* Brightly colored bird of Central and South America, with large, downward-curved beak, reminiscent of Brzezinski *after* a nose job.

tourist (TUR-ist), *n.* A sub-aboriginal species of itinerant busybodies, hunter-gadgeters, sea-going snapshooters, and salad bar-barians, when sober. Tourists are deployed in dreadnoughts called cruise ships and bulldozers and battering rams called SUVs. Commonly confused with the lesser *TAIR-ur-ist*, or one who orgasmicizes at the thought of high explosives and automatic weapons.

tournament (TOOR-nuh-munt), *n.* Originally, a mindless Medieval bloodletting not unlike hockey on horseback, although the contestants were said to be courteous and well-spoken. Currently, the term is applied to such activities as chess ("bloodletting" is appropriate if Bobby Fischer is about), golf, and parades (Tournament of Roses, etc.). *TURN-uh-mint* is the average high-sticker's grunt.

transient (TRAN-shunt, TRAN-zee-unt), *adj.* Fleeting, ephemeral, momentary, short-lived, such as upward surges in your retirement portfolio. *n.* One of the loosely employed who travels about in search of marketable skills, such as your retirement-portfolio adviser. *TRAN-zee-int* is bankrupt.

trauma (TRAW-muh, TRAU-muh), *n.* Death rudely interrupted by CPR.

triage (tree-AHZH, TREE-ahzh), *n.* In war zones, the assignment of medical treatment priorities to machine gun, bazooka, and shrapnel casualties that arrive at Receiving Hospital, St. Luke's, Bellevue, Flagler Memorial, and Highland Park General, etc. In Detroit or D.C.: *"TAKE-uh-NUM-bur."*

trilobite (TRY-luh-bite), *n.* A Paleozoic fossil, from around the time of your parents' high school graduation or your home room teacher's childhood, or about the time synchronized swimming was exciting. After your wasted college years, you, too, will pronounce it as *TRILL-uh-bite.*

t

tripartite (try-PAHR-tight), *adj*. Of three parts, or parties; a political system based on more than one philosophy, such as that of the Greens, the Independents, and the Libert-Aryans; as distinguished from a "monopartite" (*MAH-no-PAHR-tight*) or single-party system, such as the Republicans and Democrats.

triton (TRI-ton), *n*. 6,000 lbs.

tsetse (TSET-see), *n*. An insect that flies in the face of African pest control. It is the cause of several maladies including "sleeping sickness," a disease once thought by high-ranking geniuses at the CDC to be merely the result of uninspiring sermons. *TEET-see* and *SEET-see* are not neat, see?

turmeric (TUR-muh-rik), *n*. An herb. Not a difficult word except for TV chefs, who invariably pronounce it as *TOO-mur-ik*, usually in the same breath that they mispronounce the spice cumin (*KUH-mun*) as *KYOO-min* and culinary (*KULL-uh-ner-ee*) as *KYOO-luh-nair-ee*. "She'll bring cumin around th' mountain when she comes; she'll bring cumin around th' mountain when she comes. . . ." Turmeric is currently touted as a magical curative for imaginary diseases of the future.

2001 (TWO THOUSAND ONE), *n.* 1. A space oddity and all-round seminal year. 2. The number of chaps running for governor of California in 2003. 3. The number of clean-shaven males over the age of twelve in the USA. 4. The number of subscription opera tickets sold in the USA in any given decade. 5. Haitian coups since 1901. 6. The year Don King's hairdo appeared fashionable. 7. The centennial of Mike Wallace's broadcast career. *TWO THOUSAND AND ONE* is haironeous.

t

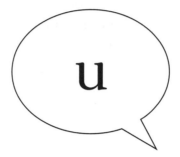

ump ire, *n*. Delay of game.

undulation (UN-juh-LAY-shun), *n*. A writhing, rolling pulsation, as in when Congress does the "wave" to the president's bump-and-grind that is demurely called the State of the Union address. *UN-doo-late* is okay, depending on what you're undoing.

unwieldy (un-WEEL-dee), *adj.* Difficult to mismanage but not impossible. *un-WEELD-lee* is unwelcome.

Uranus (yoo-RAY-nus), *n.* Seventh planet from the sun. Atmosphere is dense and gaseous. Reputed to be locality from which talk show guests are recruited. It is also the source of the words for the finals of the annual National Spelling Bee. *YUR-uh-nus* is out of this world.

u

vacuum (VAH-kyoom), *n*. Affordable housing for pea-brains, or other Aryan Brotherhoodlums, neo-Nazis, malcontents, poachers, etc. *v.t.* To use a vacuum cleaner (machine). *VAK-yoom*, popularly.

valentine (VAH-lun-tyne), *n*. A hoax perpetrated by the vast Right Wing greeting card conspiracy. Also, the emblem of the Holiday For Distraught Lovers, once *properly* celebrated in Chicago. *VAL-un-times* is a favorite of uneducable boors fondly attached to "CHIM-lee" and "LIE-berry."

valet (VAH-lut), *n.* A manservant entrusted with the misplacing of the master's gold cufflinks rather than the pilfering of his Port, which is the office of the butler. (According to Lord Chidebeek, the "r" was removed from the word quite prematurely.) In France and America, *va-LAY, pool-BOY*, or one who sees to the mistress's laundry and, on occasion, plumbing.

V

vase (VAYSS), *n.* A useless gimcrack narrower than a beanpot but taller than an ashtray and generally interfering with a proper decor. Women and art dealers hoard them, expectantly. Real men insist on vase-ectomies. *VAZE* is still somewhat user-friendly; *VAHZ* borders on snobbery (thank God), chicanery, and all that is lusted after by your ex's attorney's wife.

vegan (VEE-gun), *n.* A native of or traveler from Vega, a gaseous cloud in the constellation Lyra. (From Chicago, hang a left at St. Louis and drive until you come to a two-star Holiday Inn Express with leaky plumbing.) The gas on Vega is said to emanate from the exhaust of its inhabitants, all of whom are strict vegetarians (their leather whips, bras, and garter belts being constructed from petrified eggplant rind). *VAY-gun* is acceptable in Berkeley and Cornell.

vegetable (VEJ-tuh-b'l, VEH-juh-tuh-b'l), *n.* Anything not animal or mineral. The author's all-time favorite pronunciation is *WEJ-uh-tay-b'l*, Wolfgang Puck's priceless take, reportedly. Go, Wolfman!

vehicle (VEE-uh-k'l), *n.* A means of conveying or being taken for a ride. In the USA, a new or used motor-transport enjoying a rather distant relationship with the Truth in Mileage Act of 1986. *VEE-hik'l* has less horsepower but more hick power.

V

vehicular (vee-HIK-yuh-lur), *adj.* A popular variety of homicide.

venereal (vuh-NIR-e-ul), *adj.* Of diseases caused or transmitted by the second planet from the sun. Venus's dramatic influence on Earth is said to have begun in 1492, when Columbus repealed the blue laws in Key West. This charming word has since been displaced by "STD" to accommodate whatever it is that they're turning out in maternity wards these days.

Venus de Milo (VEE-nus duh ME-lo), *n.* A statue of limitations. A marblous Greek sculpture from about 150 B.C. and found on the island of Melos (*ME-los*) in 1820. Erroneously said to have inspired Hemingway's *A Farewell to Arms*. Popularly, *duh MY-lo*. Duh.

Venus's flytrap, *n.* Erroneously: "Venus flytrap." Popular example of carnivorous plant life; others being the bladderwort, the pitcher plant, and the middle-school freshman.

verbosity (vur-BAH-suh-tee), *n.* That which put the "moan" in "ceremony," the "unction" in "function," the "ohhh!" in "prose." A running-off at the word processor. *ver-BOE-suh-tee* is nominally short.

Veronique (vay-raw-NEEK), *n.* The *sole* of discretion. *vuh-RAHN-uh-kuh* can't come out to play.

Vespucci (veh-SPOO-chee), **Amerigo** (uh-MER-ih-go) (1451–1512). Italian navigator who lent his name to a fantasy camp for terrorists and dumping ground for corporate accounting errors, where wire fraud rules, one in four residents subscribes to the sumo diet plan, and inebriates feed the hungry three squares on Thanksgiving, Christmas, and Easter. *ves-POO-see,* media-wise.

via (VIE-uh), *prep.* By way of, as in "to Paris via Lyons" or "to the Rose Garden via lyin'." *VEE-uh* is properly used only address-wise, mainly in the southwestern USA and the barrios of Benedict Canyon.

V

viaduct (VIE-uh-dukt), *n.* A steel or masonry bridge supported by piers or towers, or, in the USA, by pork barrels. *VIE-uh-dahk* or *VIE-dahk* being the standard slippage.

Viagra (vi-AGG-ruh), *n.* No pronunciation problem here, except possibly among cage fighters, beach groupies, exercise gurus, Frat pledges, Cialas and Levitra sales reps, or anyone who would wait in line for seventy-seven hours to buy Super Bowl tickets.

Viagra, the modern "Spanish fly," was designed to cure erectile problems (in men), unless, of course, you're a prostate surgery survivor; then you get all the side effects of the drug but none of the front. Viagra comes with several cautions and warnings, such as 1. "May cause blurred vision while watching porno flicks"; 2. "Do not take with nitroglycerin tabs, as your pee-pee may explode"; and 3. "Do not place in the office water cooler on a Monday."

vicious cycle, *phr.* The correct rendering of this expression is "vicious circle," meaning, for example, a roundtable discussion involving members of a homeowners' association or pro-athlete chemical dependency committee where not *too* many felonious assaults on the rules committee take place before the coffee and steroids are served.

victual (VIH-t'l), *n.* Food; provisions. More commonly seen in the plural. A word reputedly first used in the sixteenth century by Sir Don of Rumzfeld when accused by town criers of denying food and medical supplies to Saracen children. The word was never pronounced as spelled, except during the Ford administration.

vicuña (vi-KOON-yuh), *n*. The wild camel of the Andes. Its luxurious wool is woven into icons for the retired coastal tribes of Palm Beach. *vih-KOON-uh* and *vi-KOON-uh* do not waltz with m' tilde.

Vidalia (vuh-DAIL-yuh), *adj., n*. In his annual State of the *Onion* address, the governor of Georgia, after taking a leek and shaking it contemptuously in front of the mostly Baptist audience, praised the superior Vidalia as ". . . a peach of a lily larger than a scallion that, when eaten like an apple, tastes as sweet as an onion."

Vietnam (veet-NAM, ve-et-NAM, -NAHM, etc.). A place-name having achieved immortality in diplomatic circles as a suffix of, variously, "another," "his," "their," etc. Synonym: "Demilitarized Zone."

viscosity (vis-KAH-suh-tee), *n*. Science friction.

Volvo (VOLE-vo, VAWL-vo), *n*. A Saab sister.

voyeur (vwah-YUR), *n*. One titillated or erotically aroused merely from furtively gazing upon or ogling certain body parts, especially the lines, curves, bulges,

V

etc. of a well-preserved Jaguar XKE or Ferrari Super America. *VOY-ur* for those who can't see their way clear.

V

war (WOR, WAWR), *n*. When Bush comes to shove. The sport of kings, when the stables are empty. WAR is EL in Chicago.

wash (WAHSH), *v*. To make less grimy. What's the pronunciation problem here that causes effete suburbanites to "go" *WORSH* after getting the *GROESH-reez* and picking up the kids after soccer and drug practice?

wastrel (WAYS-trul), *n.* A good-for-anything spend-thrift, such as Congress, which, on occasion, tends to make drunken sailors look downright stingy. *WAHS-trul* is worthless.

water (WAW-tur), *n.* The liquor of life, commonly awaiting distillant upgrades. Humans are notorious water wasters; therefore, clean or potable water is in short supply worldwide, especially in the south-western U.S. where, according to multiplemormon-maids@moab.com, the situation is so critical that two or more Californians are said to shower together merely in order to conserve the precious fluid. In Philadelphia and New Jersey it's pronounced *WOOD-ur*, and in Australia it's *WOO-tuh*.

werewolf (WIR-wulf), *n.* A figment of a cinematog-rapher's imagination. The second person singular, past indicative of "waswolf." Synonym: "Lon Chaney, Jr." *WUR-wolf*, popularly, as distinguished from "Dracula" or any anemic pseudointellectual basking in the prime of death (rockers).

W

Westminster (WES[T]-min-stur), *n*. A borough of London zoned for legitimate business but allowing Parliament to reside there anyway. *west-MIN-ih-stur* and *west-MIN-stur* are Low English examples from dog shows and the Bow Bells of D.C.

whale (WAYL), *n*. A large mythical "fish" (super-fish'l mammal), especially white, symbolizing Man's eternal struggle to overcome his fear of poaching. The most intelligent ingredient of shoe polish. *WAIL*, when extinct.

wit, *n*. An alternative sentimentality called "sarcasm" by ignorant fools and "flippancy" by learned ones.

Wodehouse (WOOD-house), **Pelham Grenville** (1881–1975). English-born American humorist and literary caricaturist, of "Jeeves" fame, as adamant about the pronunciation of his surname as he was about the universal truth that the biggest liars in the world are not fishermen, bankers, or barristers, but golfers. Also suggested that shot clocks be sold with sets of golf clubs. Captured by Germans during World

War II; knighted by Queen Elizabeth II in 1975, despite his collaboration with . . . New Yorkers.

women (WIH-min), *n*. A minority group whose entitlements to war, graft, credit fraud, shystering, and quackery were, until 1977, traditionally abridged. The mystery of the first syllable "ih" sound in "women" is right up there with such conundra as: Why is there no clear photo of a UFO? Do worker ants take a day off? and What would happen if Gray Davis visited Pink Floyd in Orange County parked in a red zone behind a tanning parlor during a blackout?

W

worsted (WOOS-tid), *n*. After Worstead, England. A woolen fabric originating there and lasting a minimum of a thousand years, or until Chubby Checker calls it quits. Tales that the fabric is more unyielding than Kevlar and that it once caused a Lancashire moth to visit an orthodontist are unsubstantiated.

wrestling (RESS-ling), *n*. Grappling. *RASS-lin'*, if you're rude and do it in the nude.

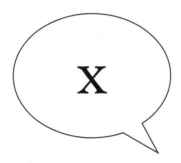

xenophobia (zeh-nuh-FO-be-uh), *n*. The third from the last phobia: fear and/or hatred of foreigners. A handy phobia to have if you're a Klansman, but *not* to have if you're a CEO secretly encouraging the illegal importation of cheap labor from Mexico to fatten up your bottom line. *ZEE-no-FO-be-uh* is incorrect, except where Zeno hangs out.

Xerxes (ZURK-seez) (circa 519–465 B.C.). King of Persia, son of Darius the Great. An active conqueror and administrator all his life, Xerxes found retirement to be murder. *ZUR-seez* is tolerable.

X

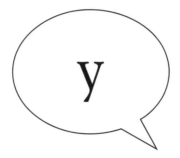

yield (YEELD), *v.t.* A word the definition of which was lost with the invention of the intersection.

Yom Kippur (yoem kih-POOR). Jewish "Day of Atonement." Holiday celebrated with fasting and prayer and occurring about ten days before the commencement of the Twelve Weeks of Christmas. *yahm KIH-pur* and *yahm kih-POOHR* are slightly fragrant but quite popular among the media *goys* and dolls.

you're (YOOHR). Contraction of "you are," as in fired, under arrest, boorish, deceptive, insensitive, certifiable, tasteless, etc., according to several renowned you'reologists. *YOAR* is certifiably common.

youths (YOOTHS), *n.* In America, an influential peer group said to peer into everything but textbooks. *YOOTS*, acceptable only from Ph.D. candidates in Grief Counseling, Sports Medicine, etc.

Y

zeitgeist (TSIGHT-guyst), *n*. German for "spirit of the times." Currently: noise, traffic, gluttony, inebriation, "the illustrated man" (with cell phone), and other cheap thrills the Rolling Stones are seriously considering when paroled from their stint in the retirement community. In other words, a zight for zore eyze.

zero (ZEAR-o), *n*. Naught, null, nil, none, as in 1. What the Swede has left over after taxes; 2. The likelihood of a referee calling "traveling" or "intentional grounding" on an NBA/NFL media darling; 3. The chances of unexpurgated U.S. history being taught (or learned) in an American high school; 4. The number of public libraries within inner-city America; 5. The dollar amount of a congressional appropriation for alternative fuel research; or 6. The odds that the "Patriot Act" is *not* the preface to a police state. *ZEE-ro*, in the Interstate 40 corridor.

Z

zinfandel (ZIN-fun-dell), *n*. In the second act of vintage TV drama *Any Old Port in a Storm*, the gifted Donald Pleasence, playing an oenophile-cum-homicido, alluded, with his usual aplomb, to a "*zin-FAND'l*" at dinner. Columbo didn't detect it.

zoology (zoh-AH-luh-jee), *n*. The biological science dealing with the classification of poachable animals and the annihilation of species. *ZOO-AH-luh-je* is for apes.

zoomorphic (zoh-uh-MOR-fik), *adj*. Pertaining to certain silly aboriginal deities having taken the form of animals, such as the humpback whale; as distinguished from our sophisticated and civilized god, the greenback.

zucchini (zoo-KEE-nee), *n.* A cucumber-shaped green summer squash, impervious to the weeding hoe and served to children at gunpoint. Synonyms: "cauliflower," "turnip," "Brussels sprout." This word is scheduled to be mispronounced on December 19, 2022, during the valedictory at Yale (by a member of the Bush league).

zymurgy (ZY-mur-jee), *n.* The ancient properties governing the slurring of speech and the wearing of lampshades. When Noah's ark is eventually found, it will show evidence of a still. (Who could blame him!) *ZY-mur-gee* is non.

zzxjoanw (????????), *n.* Close, but no, this is not the greeting heard over the drive-thru speaker at a fast food eatery. It is a Maori drum, according to eminent alternative lexicographer Mr. Peter Bowler. We'll leave the pronunciation to the Maoris, although Welshmen and Poles are said to be able to do wonders with it.

Z

ac·knowl·edg·ments

A special thanks to Dick Cavett for phoning Court TV during the Danielle Van Dam murder trial and remarking upon the four-syllable pronunciation of the word "mischievous" offered into evidence by a member of the defense team. It reminded me of where I had stashed the unfinished manuscript of this book.

A *very* special thanks to benevolent taskmaster Mr. Jofie Ferrari-Adler for his insights, able assistance, and proper prodding during the preparation of the final draft of the manuscript.